SUGARLESS—THE WAY FORWARD

Edited by

A.J. RUGG-GUNN

Professor of Preventive Dentistry, Departments of Oral Biology and Child Dental Health, University of Newcastle upon Tyne, UK

ELSEVIER APPLIED SCIENCE
LONDON and NEW YORK

ELSEVIER SCIENCE PUBLISHERS LTD
Crown House, Linton Road, Barking, Essex IG11 8JU, England

Sole Distributor in the USA and Canada
ELSEVIER SCIENCE PUBLISHING CO., INC.
655 Avenue of the Americas, New York, NY 10010, USA

WITH 23 TABLES AND 31 ILLUSTRATIONS

© 1991 ELSEVIER SCIENCE PUBLISHERS LTD
© 1991 CROWN COPYRIGHT—pp. 5–9

British Library Cataloguing in Publication Data

Sugarless — the way forward.
1. Health. Effect of sugar
I. Rugg-Gunn, Andrew J.
574.1

ISBN 1-85166-598-6

Library of Congress CIP data applied for

Printed in Great Britain at the University Press, Cambridge

v

Contents

List of Contributors vii

Introduction 1
    A.J. RUGG-GUNN

Dietary Sugars and Human Disease. Department of Health's COMA
Report: Conclusions and Recommendations 5

Sugars and Disease: The COMA Report 10
    H. KEEN

Physicochemical Properties and Applications of Sugarless Sweeteners . . . 18
    G.G. BIRCH

Metabolism and Tolerance of Sugarless Sweeteners 32
    P. WÜRSCH

Sugars, Fat and Dietary Counselling 52
    A.E. BLACK

Sugars, Sweeteners and Dental Caries Prevention 70
    M. TRILLER

Confectionery Applications and Marketing in Switzerland 85
    J.-C. SALAMIN

Sugarfree Applications and Marketing in the UK 93
    P. HAMILTON

Sugars, Sweeteners and EC Regulations 100
    P.-M. VINCENT

Sugars and Dental Health in Young Children 125
    P. HOBSON

A Survey of the Use of Liquid Oral Medicines 134
    A. MAGUIRE

Formulating Sugar-free Oral Liquid Medicines 154
   S.W. BOND and C.D. FIELDS

Prescribing Sugar-free Liquid Oral Medicines 163
   G.M. MITCHELL

Dental Health Education and Promotion 169
   F. LEDWITH

The Swiss Association for 'Tooth-Friendly' Sweets (The Sympadent
Association) 197
   T. IMFELD and B. GUGGENHEIM

vii

List of Contributors

G.G. Birch, Department of Food Science and Technology, University of Reading, Whiteknights, PO Box 226, Reading RG6 3AP, UK (p. 18)

A.E. Black, Research Dietitian, Dunn Clinical Nutrition Centre, 100 Tennis Court Road, Cambridge CB2 1QL, UK (p. 52)

S.W. Bond, Consumer Healthcare Product Development, The Wellcome Foundation Ltd, Temple Hill, Dartford, Kent DA13 0RY, UK (p. 154)

C.D. Fields, Consumer Healthcare Product Development, The Wellcome Foundation Ltd, Temple Hill, Dartford, Kent DA13 0RY, UK (p. 154)

B. Guggenheim, Department of Oral Microbiology and General Immunology, Zurich University Dental School, Plattenstrasse 11, CH-8028 Zurich, Switzerland (p. 197)

P. Hamilton, Managing Director, The Wrigley Company Ltd, Estover, Plymouth, Devon PL6 7PR, UK (p. 93)

P. Hobson, Department of Oral Health and Development, University of Manchester Dental School, Higher Cambridge Street, Manchester M15 6FH, UK (p. 125)

T. Imfeld, Department of Preventive Dentistry, Periodontology and Cariology, Zurich University Dental School, Plattenstrasse 11, CH-8028 Zurich, Switzerland (p. 197)

H. Keen, Unit for Metabolic Medicine, United Medical and Dental Schools of Guy's and St Thomas's Hospital, 4th Floor, Hunt's House, Guy's Hospital, London Bridge, London SE1 9RT, UK (p. 10)

F. Ledwith, Department of Education, University of Manchester, Oxford Road, Manchester M60, UK (p. 169)

A. Maguire, Department of Child Dental Health, University of Newcastle upon Tyne, Framlington Place, Newcastle upon Tyne NE2 4BW, UK (p. 134)

G.M. Mitchell, University of Wales College of Medicine, Heath Park, Cardiff CF4 4XN, UK (p. 163)

J.-C. Salamin, Group Product Manager/Chocolate Division, Société des Produits Nestlé SA, Case Postale 352, 1800 Vevey, Switzerland (p. 85)

M. Triller, Faculté de Chirurgie Dentaire (Paris V), 1 rue Maurice Arnoux, 92120 Montrouge, France (p. 70)

P.-M. Vincent, French Food Law Association, 'Folle Avoine', Le Brulat, 83330 Le Castellet, France (p. 100)

P. Würsch, Nestlé Research Centre, Nestec Limited, Vers-chez-les-Blanc, 1000 Lausanne-26, Switzerland (p. 32)

INTRODUCTION

An international symposium took place on 19th, 20th and 21st September 1990 in the Dental School, University of Newcastle upon Tyne. Fourteen papers were presented by speakers from three European countries, and a panel discussion was held during the final session. The symposium was attended by 130 people from nine countries, providing a mix of dentists, doctors, nutritionists, chemists, pharmacists, sociologists, and industrialists concerned with manufacturing and marketing food products.

For many years, reports on health and nutrition published in Britain and abroad, have recommended a reduction in sugar intake. In 1968, the Department of Health's Committee on Medical Aspects of Food Policy (known as the COMA committee and chaired by the Chief Medical Officer) emphasised the damaging effect to children's teeth of sugared fruit-flavoured drinks and sugared medicines. In 1978, a Department of Health discussion document (Eating for Health) recommended a reduction in sugar consumption and avoidance of sugar early in life to discourage the development of a 'sweet tooth'. Reduction in sugar consumption was also recommended in reports by the National Advisory Committee for Nutritional Education and the Royal College of Physicians (report on Obesity). In 1984, the Department of Health's COMA report on Diet and Cardiovascular Disease was published. It strongly recommended a reduction in dietary fat and that the energy deficit should be replaced by complex carbohydrates and not by sugars. The role of dietary sugars in human disease was then considered by the COMA committee and their report was published in December 1989. It was the publication of this report which was a major stimulus to organise this symposium. The conclusions and recommendations of the Department of Health COMA report on Dietary Sugars and Human Disease are reproduced in full after this Introduction. It is not only in Britain that a reduction in sugar consumption has been urged. In many countries of Europe and

North America, reductions in the consumption of fats and sugar are recommended, a view endorsed by the World Health Organisation in its document 'Healthy Nutrition'.

Whilst most reports have recommended that sugars be replaced by fibre-rich complex carbohydrates, there has been a growth in the availability and use of non-sugar sweeteners. This is a broad category of products but broadly speaking they provide sweetness without the risk of dental caries and are therefore popular with the consumer (who likes a sweet taste) and the health professional (who wishes to prevent dental caries). Industry has discovered and tested a large number of non-sugar sweeteners during the past twenty years and Government has approved the use of several - in the U.K., at present, six bulk sweeteners and five intense sweeteners are approved, and the number is likely to increase further in the next few years. The dental effects of non-sugar sweeteners has been investigated in a number of countries but a particularly useful line of research has occurred in Switzerland where a test has been developed which allows foods to be marketed as "zahnschonend" (kind to teeth) for nearly twenty years. Consumers are now able to chose products which are sweet without the risk of dental caries.

Thus, the symposium was set against a background of a need to reduce consumption of sugar, largely for the prevention of dental caries, and the wider availability of alternative, non-sugar sweeteners. The first speaker, Professor Harry Keen, reviewed the work of the COMA Panel, of which he was chairman, on Dietary Sugars and Human Disease. This was followed by two papers by Drs. Birch and Würsch on the physico-chemical properties, applications, metabolism and tolerance of sugarless sweeteners. The first session ended with a discussion on the place of sugars in the diet from the nutritionist's viewpoint by Miss Alison Black. She warned that a potential danger of decreasing sugar consumption was a rise in consumption of fats.

In this symposium, it was decided to focus on two types of sugar-rich foods - confectionery and liquid oral medicines. Confectionery was chosen because it is the biggest source of added sugars in the diets of children in this country. Confectionery is very often marketed for frequent consumption and is sometimes sticky to the teeth. Reducing the consumption of sugar-rich confectionery is, therefore, seen as an important goal in health education. The dietary causes of dental caries were reviewed by Professor Monique Triller, while the problems of manufacturing sugar-free confectionery, marketing strategies and successes were presented by Mr. Jean-Claude Salamin, who gave a continental view, and Mr. Philip Hamilton, who discussed the growth of the sugar-free chewing gum market in the U.K. Regulations governing the use of sweeteners in confectionery (and other foods) increase year by year. We were guided through current and future trends in these regulations within the European Community by Mr. Pierre Vincent.

The next session concerned liquid oral medicines. The problem of dental caries and its sequelae in the young child was emphasised by Dr. Pamela Hobson. The hazard to health is of particular concern in the medically compromised child who may be on daily medication long-term. Results of a survey to determine the size of this problem was reported by Mrs. Anne Maguire. Dr. Stephen Bond provided the pharmaceutical manufacturer's viewpoint, emphasising the many advantages of sugar and some of the difficulties of reformulating medicines without sugar. The majority of medicines are prescribed by doctors who use as a reference the British National Formulary (BNF). Dr. George Mitchell, who served on the Joint Formulary Committee of the BNF for many years, discussed the possible wider use of non-sugar sweeteners in medicines, and ways in which the number of medicines containing sugar might be reduced.

The last session was concerned with achieving reductions in sugar consumption. Dr. Frank Ledwith outlined the principles of health promotion and education, with special reference to the successful campaign recently completed in N.W. England. The health promotional aspect of this campaign was modelled on anti-smoking programmes. The last speaker, but by no means least, was Dr. Thomas Imfeld who gave a history of the development of a system for testing the cariogenicity of food products and an account of the Swiss association for tooth-friendly sweets. This association has now become international with branches in Germany and France. It is also known as the Sympadent Association, and has as a protected symbol, the smiling molar-man. This symbol is recognised, by children especially, as an indication that this confectionery is safe for teeth. The symposium ended with a panel discussion during which the hopes, anxieties and successes of those in industry were freely expressed.

The order of the papers in these Proceedings follows the order in which papers were given at the symposium. The contents of the published papers are virtually the same as the oral presentations, and there has been minimal editing. I would like to thank all the speakers for preparing manuscripts of their most interesting papers, and for travelling to Newcastle, joining in the discussions and ensuring the success of the meeting. The sessions were chaired by four professors in the University of Newcastle Medical Faculty - I thank John Murray, George Alberti and Mike Rawlins for assisting me in this task. I wish, also, to thank Miss Karen Short for her typing skills, and Mr. Peter Desmond of Elsevier Applied Science Publishers for his advice and assistance in publishing these Proceedings. The organisation of the meeting fell on the shoulders of Mrs. Anne Maguire. I thank her and the staff of the Departments of Child Dental Health and Oral Biology, University of Newcastle upon Tyne, for their great assistance.

The symposium was designed to provide a forum for diverse groups of experts to discuss the possibilities of removing sugar from certain dietary itmes so as to reduce the threat to dental health. These exchanges of views were necessary if progress is to continue. Publication of these Proceedings will refresh the memories of those who attended, and will be a valuable source of reference to those unable to attend. It also forms a bench-mark against which further progress towards a sugarless future may be measured.

A.J. R-G.

DIETARY SUGARS AND HUMAN DISEASE

Department of Health. Report on Health and Social Subjects 37.
Committee on Medical Aspects of Food Policy. Report of the
Panel on Dietary Sugars.   HMSO, December 1989.

CHAPTER 14

CONCLUSIONS AND RECOMMENDATIONS

14.1   The Panel's remit was to review the evidence relating
sugars in the diet to health.

14.2   The Panel found no evidence that the consumption of most
sugars naturally incorporated in the cellular structure
of foods (intrinsic sugars) represented a threat to
health.   Consideration was therefore mainly directed
towards the dietary use of sugars not so incorporated
(extrinsic sugars).   Non-milk extrinsic sugars,
principally sucrose, at present constitute about 15
to 20 per cent of the average daily food energy supply
in the UK.

14.3   **Dental caries**

14.3.1   Dental caries remains prevalent in the UK.   It is of
social, medical and economic importance.   Extensive
evidence suggests that sugars are the most important
dietary factor in the cause of dental caries.   Their
presence at plaque-covered tooth surfaces is essential
for more than very limited caries development.   Caries
experience is positively related to the amount of non-
milk extrinsic sugars in the diet and the frequency of
their consumption.   Staple starchy foods, intrinsic
sugars in whole fruit and milk sugars are negligible

causes of dental caries. Non-sugar bulk and intense sweeteners are non-cariogenic or virtually so. A reduction in the consumption of non-milk extrinsic sugars would be expected further to reduce the prevalence of dental caries in the UK.

14.3.2 Dental caries can occur at any age but those at greatest risk are children, adolescents and the elderly. Caries risk can be reduced by non-dietary means, particularly the use of fluoride, but these methods offer incomplete protection and some are expensive.

14.3.3 In order to reduce the risk of dental caries, the Panel recommends that consumption of non-milk extrinsic sugars by the population should be decreased. These sugars should be replaced by fresh fruit, vegetables and starchy foods.

14.3.4 Those providing food for families and communities should seek to reduce the frequency with which sugary snacks are consumed.

14.3.5 For infants and young children simple sugars (e.g. sucrose, glucose, fructose) should not be added to bottle feeds; sugared drinks should not be given in feeders where they may be in contact with the teeth for prolonged periods; dummies or comforters should not be dipped in sugars or sugary drinks.

14.3.6 Older children need to be aware of the importance of diet and nutrition in relation to dental as well as general health. The Panel recommends that schools should promote healthy eating patterns both by nutrition education and by providing and encouraging nutritionally sound food choices.

14.3.7 Elderly people with teeth should restrict the amount and frequency of consumption of non-milk extrinsic sugars because their teeth are more likely to decay due to exposure of tooth roots and declining salivary flow.

14.3.8 An increasing number of liquid medicines are available in 'sugar free' formulations. When medicines are needed, particularly long-term, such alternatives should

be selected by parents and medical practitioners.
The Panel recommends that Government should seek the
means to reduce the use of sugared liquid medicines.

14.3.9 Dental practitioners should give dietary advice,
including reduction of non-milk extrinsic sugars
consumption, as an important part of their health
education to patients, particularly to those who are
especially prone to dental caries. To facilitate this,
the Panel recommends that teaching of nutrition during
dental training should be increased, and professional
relations between dietitians and dental practitioners be
encouraged.

14.4 **Obesity**

14.4.1 Dietary sugars may contribute to the general excess
food energy consumption responsible for the development
of obesity. This condition plays an important part in
the aetiology of a number of diseases, e.g. diabetes,
raised blood pressure, hyperlipidaemia and arterial
disease and gallstones.

14.4.2 Omission of sugars from the diet, though safe, is not
usually sufficient as a weight reducing regimen.
Restriction of fats in the diet is also important in
reducing obesity and has other health advantages. The
Panel endorses the need for the obese to reduce energy
consumption and recommends that the reduction of non-
milk extrinsic sugars intake should be part of a general
reduction in dietary energy intake. Overweight people
who wish to lose weight and those becoming obese should
follow the same approach to dietary energy restriction
as that recommended for obese people. The Panel
recommends intensification of research into the
determinants of food choices and the mechanisms of the
variety of individual responses to food intakes.

14.5 **Metabolism**

14.5.1 There is no evidence for a direct adverse effect in most people on blood levels of cholesterol, triglycerides, glucose or insulin when sucrose is substituted isocalorically for starch up to about 150 g per day or 25 per cent of total food energy. A subgroup, possibly genetically determined and often overweight, comprising 10 to 15 per cent of the population, may respond with hyperlipidaemia to high normal intakes of sugars. At high levels of sucrose intake (about 200 g per day or 30 per cent of food energy) substituted isocalorically for starch, undesirable elevations may occur in fasting plasma lipids, insulin and glucose.

14.5.2 A relatively small group of people with metabolic disorders may need to restrict or regulate their intake of particular sugars. This includes people with diabetes and those with certain rare inherited disorders.

14.5.3 For the majority of the population, who have normal plasma lipids and normal glucose tolerance, the consumption of sugars within the present range in the UK carries no special metabolic risks. Those members of the population consuming more than about 200 g per day should replace the excess with starch. The Panel recommends that those with special medical problems such as diabetes and hypertriglyceridaemia should restrict non-milk extrinsic sugar intake to less than about 25 to 50 g per day unless otherwise instructed by their own physician or dietitian.

14.6 Links between sucrose intake and certain other diseases (e.g. colo-rectal cancer, renal and biliary calculi, Crohn's disease) have been proposed. Although the Panel did not feel the evidence was adequate to justify any general dietary recommendations, it recommends the intensification of research in these areas. The Panel recommends that human nutrition should form an integral part of the training of medical students and of other health professionals.

14.7   The Panel concluded that current consumption of sugars, particularly sucrose, played no direct causal role in the development of cardiovascular (atherosclerotic coronary, peripheral or cerebral vascular) disease, of essential hypertension, or of diabetes mellitus (either insulin-dependent or non-insulin dependent). It further concluded that sucrose had no significant specific effects on behaviour or psychological function.

14.8   Artificial and alternative sweeteners can be considered non-cariogenic or virtually so and are useful sugar substitutes within limits prescribed by other Expert Advisory Committees. The Panel recommends that food manufacturers produce 'low sugars' or 'sugars-free' alternatives to existing sugar-rich products, particularly those for children.

14.9   Those wishing to regulate their sugars consumption need information of the sugars content of foods. The Panel recommends that manufacturers adopt current proposals for labelling foods including their total sugars content. The Panel further recommends that the Government seek the means for analysis and labelling of non-milk extrinsic sugars if practicable.

14.10   The Panel recommends that the Government should monitor average and extreme intakes of non-milk extrinsic sugars by members of the population in relation to the general and dental health of the public.

SUGARS AND DISEASE
The COMA Report

H KEEN
Professor of Human Metabolism
Unit for Metabolic Medicine
UMDS – Guy's Campus, London SE1 9RT, UK

INTRODUCTION

When changes in human culture occur together, the question inevitably arises of causal links between them. This is perhaps particularly true when health and disease are concerned. Improved sanitation, nutrition, education and communication, along with therapeutic discovery have led to the control of infectious disease and consequent prolongation of life expectancy. This has brought the non communicable disorders to greatly increased clinical prominence. Hypertension, atherosclerotic arterial disease with heart attack, stroke and gangrene, cancer, diabetes and mental disorder are now the leading causes of chronic ill-health and early death in industrialised societies. Major nutritional changes have occurred over roughly the same time span with both an overall increase in the availability of foods and alterations in the composition of the average human diet. On the basis of simple association and other evidence of variable quality, certain of these nutritional changes have been proposed as responsible for, or contributory to, the rise of the non-communicable diseases. A correlation in time between nutritional change and rising disease prevalence does not establish a cause and effect relationship, but neither does it exclude it.

The clear lesson from the conquest of the communicable disease was the crucial importance of prevention. This has set the tone for the attack on the non communicable diseases and fostered the search for preventable nutritional causes. There are plausible biological links and sometimes supporting experimental evidence but simple causal hypotheses are often proposed - and resisted - more with fervour than with fact. There are very strong economic, cultural and emotional forces vested in food production and consumption and these explain, to some extent, the heat with which these arguments are sometimes pursued.

THE PANEL ON DIETARY SUGARS

Sugars, a substantial contributor to average daily food energy intake in UK citizens, have been the subject of debate for decades. Assertions, claims and counterclaims have given rise to confusion and uncertainty. In recent years, expert groups have reviewed the evidence and made pronouncements and recommendations.

In 1986, the Committee on the Medical Aspects of Food Policy (COMA) convened a panel of experts to review the conflicting evidence on the role of dietary sugars in human disease and to make recommendations. The Panel included nutritionists, physicians, dental experts, biochemists and a psychiatrist. It met 10 times over 2 years and considered dietary sugars consumption in relation to a broad spectrum of disease.

The Panel felt it wished to distinguish between "intrinsic" sugars, i.e. soluble carbohydrates integrated within the structure of foods, essentially within unruptured plant cell walls, and those not so confined, which they termed "extrinsic", a group which was further subdivided into "recipe" and "table" sugars. Milk sugars were treated as a special case. With some minor reservations the Panel concluded that no health hazard attached to intrinsic sugars.

SUGARS CONSUMPTION IN BRITAIN

The contribution of sugars in their various forms, but mainly as
sucrose, to the human diet grew rapidly from the middle of the
19th century to constitute, in the 1960's, almost one fifth (80-
90% of it sucrose) of the food energy available for human
consumption. From that peak the proportion has fallen to about
one seventh, mainly from a reduction in sucrose, most of it
packet sugar. It was during these post-war years that a growing
number of claims was made that high sugars consumption was
linked with a number of disease states, including dental caries,
diabetes mellitus, disease of heart and arteries, obesity and
disordered behaviour. These disorders were attributed either to
a direct effect of the sugars themselves, or to the dietary
depletion of natural fibre associated with the use of refined
carbohydrate.

SUGARS AND DENTAL CARIES

The Panel considered evidence of many types on the relationship
between sugars and dental caries. Clinical trials,
epidemiological observations, experiments in animals and
laboratory studies provided convergent evidence that soluble
sugars created local conditions around the teeth favouring the
growth of microorganisms which produced acid metabolites from
the sugars and dissolution of tooth enamel. Sucrose, glucose,
fructose and maltose could all serve as substrates, but lactose
in milk and complex carbohydrates were much less cariogenic.
Other factors such as inherent susceptibility, frequency of
sugar ingestion, use of fluoride and dental care also appeared
to play a modifying role. The young and the old appeared most
at risk. The Panel concluded that further reduction of dental
caries in Britain required reduction in the consumption of non-
milk extrinsic sugars.

METABOLIC ASPECTS OF SUGARS CONSUMPTION

The effects of sugars after absorption appeared, in large part, to be related to the speed they entered the circulation from the intestine. The rise and fall of blood glucose as carbohydrate is absorbed is associated with a reciprocal rise and fall in insulin concentration. Raised insulin levels are held by some to predispose to arterial disease though the evidence for this is not conclusive. Alterations in plasma lipids creating a "lipid profile" associated with increased risk of arterial disease has been attributed to high intake of sugars, but the evidence of a sustained elevation of cholesterol (in low density lipoproteins) or triglycerides (in very low density and/or intermediate density lipoproteins) is not very secure. It has been suggested that there may be a "sugar-sensitive" subgroup of individuals with exaggerated insulin and lipid responses to sugar intake but it is difficult to exclude the confounding effects of obesity in interpreting these responses. The evidence suggested that it was only with intakes in excess of 200g/day that potentially advserse metabolic responses might be provoked. With a mean population intake of about 120g/d/head, only a small proportion of the population exceed this level and they were counselled to reduce sugars and replace them with unrefined carbohydrate.

SUGARS INTAKE AND OBESITY

This question was central to the Panel's discussions. The obese are more liable to a variety of important conditions such as diabetes mellitus, raised blood pressure and hyperlipidaemia with adverse consequences in respect of coronary, peripheral and cerebral artery disease, so that if sugars intake is specially linked with obesity it will indirectly contribute to its consequences.

All energy-containing nutrients will contribute to obesity, the evidence of a net energy intake in excess of expenditure. Theoretically, sugars might contribute specially to obesity in three ways. First, the energy cost associated with sugars intake might be lower than with other isocaloric nutrients.

There was no direct evidence for this and the calculated difference in thermogenesis from protein consumption was very small. Secondly, energy from sugars intake might be selectively steered towards fat synthesis; again sound evidence for this was lacking. Third, there might be some properties of sugars that encourage their overconsumption without a reciprocal reduction in other food energy sources. Most published work on diet and obesity provides little evidence that the obese consume more sugar than the non-obese; some population studies in fact suggest the contrary. The relationship between food energy intake generally on the one hand, energy expenditure on the other and the liability to obesity is notoriously difficult to investigate and is still the scene of conflicting evidence. The Panel were well aware of the difficulties inherent in collecting valid data on past food consumption and even present dietary habits. There appears to be systematic underestimation when people are asked to keep a diary-type record of food intake and this recording shortfall may be greater in the obese. Patterns of energy expenditure may change while energy intake does not. Automatic adjustment of the intake of other energy-rich nutrients when the intake of one (e.g. sugars) is deliberately but covertly altered appears to be incomplete, but so it is if fat intake in increased. This important area of nutrition is clearly in need of intensified research and the Panel said so. Despite doubts about a causal role for dietary sugars in obesity, the Panel agreed that their restriction could be a useful part of a regimen of general reduction in food energy intake necessary for the correction of obesity, but was unlikely in itself to be sufficient.

DIABETES AND CARDIOVASCULAR DISEASE

It was in the area of coronary heart disease, peripheral and cerebral arterial disease that some of the most vigorous early assertions about the effects of sugars consumption, sucrose in particular, were made. The case rested heavily upon apparent epidemiological correlations when sugars consumption in different countries was set against corresponding estimates of cardiovascular mortality rates. This correlation has many exceptions and sugars consumption is so closely linked with many other dietary and socioeconomic factors that it is difficult to separate out their possible individual effects. Sugar and fat intake are closely related to each other; it was the latter nutrient that the COMA Panel on Diet and Cardiovascular Disease concluded was the more likely culprit. Within populations, evidence for a direct link between dietary sugars and cardiovascular disease is at best unconvincing and often totally unsupported.

The fundamental abnormality of diabetes mellitus, a raised blood glucose concentration would, _ab initio_ apparently suggest a causal role for excessive sugar consumption. The published evidence does not sustain that view. In respect of both of these major disease areas, recent expert reports have all agreed in exculpating sugars as a direct cause and this was the case for the Panel.

BEHAVIOUR DISORDERS AND OTHER DISEASES

Sugars have been credited with great powers in determining human mood and behaviour. The use of sweets to pacify or reward children may contribute to this. Overshoot of blood glucose levels into the hypoglycaemia range after ingestion of rapidly absorbed carbohydrate in drinks or foods has been blamed by some for mood change and other symptoms suggesting sympathetic activation, such as sweating, tremulousness, light-headedness and palpitations. Although people with such symptoms are sometimes found to show these swings of blood glucose, often they do not. Routine surveys have brought to light may people with dramatic falls in blood glucose of this sort but who are totally unaware of them. Overvigorous and unremitting activity in children the "hyperkinetic syndrome" has been attributed to sugars in the diet, sometimes in very small quantities but the Panel could find no acceptable evidence of a true association.

The Panel also reviewed evidence of links between sugars intake and biliary and renal calculi but found the relationship confounded by obesity. A history of obesity also entered into the question of a possible relationship with cancers of large bowel and breast. No evidence of a direct link was found. The rare inborn errors of metabolism such as deficiency of intestinal disaccharidases, fructosaemia and galactosaemia represent clear indications to avoid the appropriate dietary sugars.

RECOMMENDATIONS

For dental caries prevention there was an unequivocal recommendation to reduce the consumption of non-milk extrinsic sugars and to replace them with unrefined carbohyrate foods and to use artificial sweetners for taste. The frequency of sugary snack intake should be reduced and sugars removed from infant bottle feeds and paediatric medicines. The importance of education in caries prevention at school, in the home, as part of professional training and by dental practitioners was highlighted.

In obesity, the Panel proposed restriction of dietary sugar as part of weight reducing regimens. It counsels however against the risk of replacing dietary carbohydrate with fat as running counter to advice on heart disease prevention.

The Panel could find no evidence of metabolic disturbance when sugars isocalorically replaced starches up to about 150g/day or 25 per cent of total food energy. Levels of sucrose intake exceeding 200g/day could be associated with "undesirable" metabolic responses.

Special groups would need to exclude sugars (or a specific sugar) from the diet or (for instance people with diabetes) to restrict intake to 25-50g/day.

There were areas of uncertainty about the role of sugars in some human diseases and intensified research into these was recommended.

The need for information by the consumer was recognised by the recommendation to manufacturers to include total sugars content, and to Government to seek means of stating quantity of non milk extrinsic sugars.

CONCLUSION

The COMA Report on Dietary Sugars, in broad terms endorsed the views of other expert bodies, largely exculpating sugars as a direct cause of some major diseases like diabetes and coronary heart disease. However evidence for the role of sugars in dental caries is compelling and justified the recommendations that were made. The "cause" of obesity remains at one and the same time very obvious - an accumulated excess of energy consumption over energy expenditure - and a total mystery - why some people and not others? One could totally remove sugars from the human diet without harm, but, to some at least, how boring that would be.

The brief account above is drawn from the Department of Health
Report on Health and Special Subjects 37.
Dietary Sugars and Human Disease.
Report of the Panel on Dietary Sugars.
Committee on Medical Aspects of Food Policy
Her Majesty's Stationery Office, London
All relevant literature references will be found therein (Pages
45-58)

PHYSICOCHEMICAL PROPERTIES AND
APPLICATIONS OF SUGARLESS SWEETENERS

GORDON G. BIRCH
Dept of Food Science and Technology
PO Box 226, University of Reading,
Whiteknights, Reading RG6 3AP, UK

ABSTRACT

The physicochemical properties of sweeteners are outlined
and explained and their importance in governing taste
quality, taste intensity and essential technological quality
of sweeteners is indicated.   Particularly important are
the physicochemical properties in aqueous solution which allow
the behaviour and applicability of sweeteners to be understood
at the molecular level. Sweeteners possess polar, hydrophilic
and steric characteristics which may determine the stability
of their crystal lattices, solubility and hydration behaviour
in water.   The latter in turn governs packing characteristics
of sweet solute molecules in water which means their
compatibility with water structure. When the interaction
of sapid substances with water structure is studied in detail,
important relationships between solution properties and
taste quality begin to emerge and this approach may lead to a
deeper understanding of taste transduction mechanisms at the
receptor level. Physicochemical properties are also important
to assess the optimum form of a sweetener in a food
preparation.   They also determine osmotic and other
colligative properties which are relevant to food processing
and storage requirements.

INTRODUCTION

Physicochemical properties of sweeteners have frequently been determined and catalogued as an obvious prerequisite to their applications and use. Indeed the very methodology which is employed to study sweeteners is circumscribed by their intrinsic physicochemical properties and it is by these same properties that the (sometimes fine) distinction between 'sugars' and 'sugarless sweeteners' are first made. In the food world the term 'sugar' is mainly applied to cane or beet sugar (sucrose) but water-soluble carbohydrate sweeteners, according to UK legislation, have been embraced by the formula $C_x(H_2O)_y$ which, for example, includes glucose, fructose, maltose and the less common xylose (wood sugar) and trehalose (mushroom sugar). The position of these latter two sugars as food ingredients is not altogether clear but it is interesting that, according to UK legislation, sugars are not classed as sweeteners.

Moreover, the formula $C_x(H_2O)y$ excludes deoxy sugars, amino sugars and many other chemically-accepted types of sugar and it is difficult to find a concise chemical definition of sugars as a class of compound.

Sucrose tends always to be the yardstick by which all sweeteners are judged. Therefore the physicochemical properties of sweeteners seem to make them more or less similar to sucrose in their taste and behaviour in food products. If a sweetener is widely different from sucrose in its physico-chemical properties, these may have to be modified (possibly by inclusion of an additional ingredient) in order to render that sweetener acceptable to the manufacturer or consumer.

Physicochemical properties are important in the taste, texture, storage quality and economy of sugarless sweeteners and may also govern some important physiological consequences of their use.

WHAT ARE PHYSICOCHEMICAL PROPERTIES?

Physicochemical properties of sweeteners may be regarded as those physical properties of sweeteners which are attributable to their chemical architecture (Table 1) and the total numbers of such molecules in solution. They include the physical

TABLE 1
Typical physiocochemical properties

Property	Origin
Melting Point	Stability of Crystal Lattice (H-bonding etc)
Solubility on Water	Hydrophilicity. Stability of crystals toward water
Osmotic Pressure	Total number of molecules in solution
Density in Solution	Packing of solute molecules in solvent
Viscosity in Water	Hydrodynamic volume of solute
Optical Rotation	Intrinsic asymmetry of solute molecules (in solution)

properties of powdered or crystalline forms of sweeteners (which govern the preparation and use of such sweeteners in food products) and the physicochemical properties of solutions of sweeteners, usually in water. These latter may be termed solution properties and are particularly relevant to the taste, rheological characteristics and possibly the physiological effects of sweeteners.

Physicochemical properties of sweeteners in solution (i.e. solution properties) may result from a small amount of sweetener in a large amount of water (intense sweeteners) or a large amount of sweetener in a relatively small amount of water (bulk sweeteners). The former are measurable physico-chemical properties which reflect changes in the structure and properties of water by a small amount of solute whereas the latter are properties attributable to the relative amounts of free and immobilised water in the bulk sweetener system.

WHY ARE PHYSICOCHEMICAL PROPERTIES IMPORTANT IN SWEETENERS?

Physicochemical properties are important because they govern the taste and applicability of particular sweeteners in foods and medicines. Indeed the initial preparation and purification of sweeteners depends on their availability as clear, concentrated aqueous solutions (syrups) or as crystals, and the keeping quality of such preparations often depends on their hygroscopicity and osmotic pressures.

Of major importance in the food industry are elevation of the boiling point and depression of the freezing point which are colligative properties and therefore chiefly of relevance to bulk sweeteners. These properties may govern the degree of sterilisation applicable in a food preparation and its subsequent freezing (e.g. ice cream) characteristics.

The densities of powdered or crystalline sugars or their derivatives are always around $1.5g/cm^3$ whereas the density of their aqueous solutions ranges from 1.0 to about $1.4g/cm^3$. Density may not match viscosity, which depends on the tangling of hydrated solute molecules in motion (hydrodynamic volume). Viscosity is important in both the manufacture and mouthfeel of sweetened food products. It is also relatable to certain organoleptic characteristics, such as 'body','mouthfeel' and 'stickiness'. Stickiness, for example, is probably a disadvantage in fermentable sweeteners (1) if cariogenicity is to be avoided. Therefore the intense sweeteners, with no such rheological characteristics may then be the ones of choice.

Solid sweeteners may be obtained by crystallisation or evaporation of a solution to an amorphous (sometimes referred to as microcrystalline) or vitreous (glassy) state. Modern evaporation technology may allow the non-crystalline forms of sweeteners to be prepared with different bulk densities which is obviously useful for table-top applications and probably also for medicinal purposes. The crystalline form, however,

will generally have the advantage of greater intrinsic purity.
Recrystallisation could produce sweeteners matching the purity
of sucrose (>99.9%). It is important to note, however, that
the rate of dissolution of crystalline and non-crystalline
forms of a sweetener may be quite different due to
differences in the accessibility, of the crystal lattice or
microcrystalline aggregates, to water molecules. Also
different sweetener crystals may possess different heats of
solution so the process of dissolving sweetener crystals
in the mouth may cause heating or cooling effects. Xylitol,
for example, is renowned for a marked cooling effect as the
crystals dissolve. Most physicochemical properties of
sweeteners, which are important in foods, are those which
appear in water solution (solution properties). As these
depend on an intimate relationship between the sweetener
molecules and water structure they deserve special attention.

SOLUTION PROPERTIES AND THEIR RELEVANCE TO SWEETENERS

Water possesses a unique 'structure' (2) (3) (4) but the
profound details of water structure are only yet emerging (5).
It is hydrogen-bonded and,after a sweetener is dissolved, the
hydrogen-bond structure of water is disrupted. For a sweetener
to be dissolved at all it must, in some degree, be compatible
with water structure. However, it appears that those
substances with the greatest affinity for water (hydrophilic)
are those which disrupt its structure the most. For example,
salts and certain acids are very hydrophilic and therefore
disrupt water structure more than most sweeteners do. It is
therefore fairly straightforward to distinguish salty and acid
substances by some of their solution properties (e.g.
dissociation constants) but can the sweeteners be distinguished
as a chemical class, simply by solution properties? This is
a challenging question which must await more detailed understanding of solute/solvent interactions. Its answer offers
the additional prize of the distinction between sweeteners
themselves, e.g. by degree of sweetness.

The most widely accepted chemical explanation of the
phenomenon of sweetness is the hydrogen-bonding theory of
Shallenberger and Acree (6). According to this theory,
sweetness originates in those molecules which possess an AH,B
grouping (where A and B are each electronegative atoms
separated by about 2.86 Å; AH constitutes a proton donor and
B an acceptor). An AH,B grouping in a sweetener molecule
can form a reciprocal H-bonded complex with a similar AH,B
grouping on a receptor protein and this complex formation
initiates the sweetness sensation. The AH,B theory of
Shallenberger and Acree (6) is accepted by many chemists
working on the synthesis of sweeteners and AH,B groupings
can be identified. For example, the 3,4-α-glycol system of
glucopyranoside types of structure appears to be responsible
for their sweetness (7) (8). Unfortunately, however, several
molecules possessing AH,B groupings are not sweet, so the
theory is not predictive. Nevertheless hydrogen-bonding seems
to be a logical mechanism for sweet taste chemoreception, and
it explains the low-energy binding of stimulus molecule with
receptor at the peripheral stage of the transduction process.

When a solid sweetener is dissolved in water it interacts
(in the process of dissolution) with water molecules and may
disrupt the hydrogen-bonding of water molecules to a greater
or lesser degree. Finally the sweet solute molecules are
packed into the water structure and the 'degree of fit' of
the solute governs many important solution properties relevant
to its application and use. The compatibility of sweet solute
with water structure determines its packing characteristics
and one fundamentally important property is the apparent
molar volume (ϕ_V). This is defined as follows:-

$$\phi_V = MWt \frac{(1/\rho_S - Ww/\rho_w)}{Ws}$$

where ρ_S = Density of solution

ρ_w = Density of water

W_S = Weight fraction of solute

W_w = Weight fraction of water

The apparent molar volume of a solute is not constant but tends to higher values as concentration increases in water, as solute-solute interaction replaces solute-solvent interaction. For chemical purposes, values at zero concentration (infinite dilution) are computed, but these are not relevant to those concentrations of sweetener normally encountered in food formulations (e.g. 5-10% sucrose).

Although apparent molar volume is only one of several solution properties its importance as a predictor of taste quality has already been stressed (9). If apparent molar volume is converted to apparent specific volume, by dividing ϕ_V by molecular weight, the resulting apparent specific volumes provide a broad basis for categorising taste quality (Table 2).

TABLE 2

Apparent specific volume (ASV) ranges
and taste quality

ASV (cm^3g^{-1})	Taste Quality
0.1 - 0.3	Salty
0.3 - 0.5	Sour
0.5 - 0.7	Sweet
0.7 - 0.9	Bitter

It can be seen from Table 2 that molecules with apparent specific volumes ranging from 0.5 - 0.7 cm^3g^{-1} should be sweet. However, this will not be true if the molecule does not possess an appropriate "glucophore". The "glucophore" or molecular feature conferring sweetness is an AH,B system (see above). Table 2 should therefore be read with this proviso. Moreover, Table 2 shows that the sweeteners (over all sweet chemical classes) fit within the band of ASVs of 0.5 - 0.7 cm^3g^{-1}. The sugars, being the best known of the sweeteners, actually fit within a very narrow zone (0.60 - 0.62 cm^3g^{-1}) at the centre of this band and it is possible that departure from this central zone could con-stitute one reason for differences in taste quality among sweeteners.

The apparent molar volume of a sweet solute may be regarded as a resultant of two opposite factors, (i) the simple displacement of water molecules by solute molecules and (ii) electro-striction or "shrinkage" of water structure due to hydration (10). Only heavily hydrated molecules, such as sugars, acids and salts cause electrostriction. Thus heavily hydrated solutes exhibit small apparent molar volumes. It is important to note, however, that hydrophilicity is not the same as compatibility with water structure and it is the latter which is the prime determinant of apparent molar volume.

It is reasonable to anticipate that the different solution properties of sweeteners are valuable in some way. Intrinsic viscosities also yield volumes of sweeteners though these are often two to four times larger than apparent molar volumes. The reason for the difference is that viscosities represent hydrodynamic volumes whereas apparent molar volumes reflect packing characteristics in a hydrostatic state.

TYPES OF SUGARLESS SWEETENER AND THEIR SOLUTION BEHAVIOUR

Although thousands of sugarless sweeteners are now known less than twenty are permitted for food use. The sweeteners span so many different chemical classes that it is difficult to categorise them either chemically or physically. Techno-logically they may conveniently be divided into intense and bulk sweeteners, the former being 1-2 orders of magnitude greater in sweetening power, and only small amounts of them are therefore used in foods. The picture is more complicated by different chemical forms of one sweetener being available. Saccharin, for example, is allowed in the U.K. either as the free acid or its sodium or calcium salt and vast differences are immediately apparent in the solubility of these different forms. Sodium saccharin is very soluble in water (lg dissolves in 1.5ml water at 25°C or 50ml of ethanol) whereas saccharin itself (free acid) is much less soluble (lg requires 290ml water for dissolution at 25°C but only 30ml of ethanol).

The vast difference in water-solubilities between saccharin
and its sodium salt are contrastable with their similarity
in ethanol-solubilities and the cause of this phenomenon is
entirely ascribable to the hydration of the sodium salt,
which in turn gives rise to a low apparent specific volume
for sodium saccharin (ca 0.52 cm^{3}g^{-1}) at the bottom of the
sweetness range (Table 2).   Obviously, in the applications
of sweeteners in foods, it is highly convenient for a manufacturer to have a soluble form of sweetener available for an
acid medium such as a soft drink formulation.   On the other
hand, for the monitoring of saccharin levels in foods by
classical quality control procedures, the different hydro-
philicities of saccharin and its sodium salt in buffered systems
is harnessed for analytical purposes (11).   The newer intense
sweetener,acesulfame-K, is also a salt-structured substance
with a low apparent specific volume and good solubility.
It has the advantage of good taste and stability
characteristics (12).

By far the most popular of the intense sweeteners is aspartame,
a dipeptide sweetener of excellent taste though different from
sucrose. Aspartame possesses similar physicochemical
properties as other amino acid and peptide sweeteners. As
a class these substances are more polar and more hydrophobic
than the sugars and polyols. They therefore exhibit
differences in physicochemical properties at different pHs
which might cause loss of stability in acid systems. As a
class the amino acids have been extensively studied,
especially in regard to their $\underline{D}$ and $\underline{L}$ enantiomorphs. Many
literature reports suggest that the former are sweet and the
latter are bitter. However, this is a gross oversimplification
since probably most low molecular weight amino acids are sweet
(13) regardless of which enantiomer and only certain high
molecular weight $\underline{L}$-forms are bitter, as well as $\underline{D}$-proline,
which is paradoxically predominantly bitter. As a class the
amino acids are much more structurally diverse than either
the sugars or polyols and this diversity is reflected in the

broad span of their solution properties (13). The apparent
specific volumes of the amino acids, for example, range from
about 0.5 - 0.9 cm^3g^{-1} whereas sugars fit mostly within the
range 0.60 - 0.62 cm^3g^{-1}. A similar difference exists for
the range of intrinsic viscosities between the two classes
(14). Most taste panellists can perceive two, three or all
four basic tastes in any one amino acid solution (13) and this
is probably why the sweetness of amino acids is perceived as
different from that of the polyols or sugars. Actually, none
of the simple amino acids are permitted as sweeteners but
glycine, for example, (though sweet) is permitted in the U.K.
as an acidulant.

There are many chemical classes of sweetener (15) and almost
all are more hydrophobic than the sugars or polyols.
Hydrophobicity is an important physicochemical property
and is generally regarded as essential for intense sweetness.
It is determined, for example, by the octanol water partition
coefficient and, as in all drug (or stimulus)/receptor interaction, hydrophobicity may govern accession to the lipid cell
membrane. However, the generation of intense sweetness by
hydrophobicity may give rise to differences in the perceived
"quality" of sweetness for the reason advanced above. Many
amino acids are perceived as both sweet and bitter if their
apparent specific volumes (and hydrophobicities) are
sufficiently great, especially those in the border region of
the basic tastes (0.71 cm^3g^{-1}) shown in Table 2.

The one class of sweeteners which closely resemble the sugars
in many ways are the polyols (i.e. hydrogenated sugars).
The similarity is entirely attributable to their polyhydroxy
character and many of their physicochemical properties have
already been recorded (16).

THE PARTICULAR IMPORTANCE OF POLYOLS AS SUGARLESS SWEETENERS

The hydrogenation of a monosaccharide causes disruption of its
cyclic hemiacetal structure and is accompanied by a sharp
numerical drop in its specific rotation. Apart from this

difference and the absence of a free reducing centre, the polyols closely resemble the sugars in all their physico-chemical properties and taste. Thus solubilities, viscosities, osmotic pressures and refractive indices of polyols are close to those of the sugars and Kearsley (17) has used these last two properties to determine "effective DEs" of hydrogenated glucose syrups. An additional advantage of the Kearsley technique is that the DEs of normal glucose syrups can be determined much more rapidly than by the classical Lane and Eynon procedure.

Although the solution densities, and hence apparent specific volumes of the polyols, are similar to those of the parent sugars, there is an importance difference. Whereas the sugars' apparent specific volumes fit within the narrow zone $0.60 - 0.62$ cm^3g^{-1}, the simple polyols range from about $0.65-0.68$ cm^3g^{-1}, i.e. some 10% higher than the sugars. This in no way affects their sweet quality which is almost indistinguishable from the sugars (see Table 2) but it means that the polyols are less compatible with water structure than are the sugars and this must be due to loss of their cyclic structure rather than loss of the anomeric centre because myoinositol has a low apparent specific volume (9). Table 3 summarises the ranges of apparent specific volumes

TABLE 3

Sweetener class and ranges of apparent specific volumes (ASVs)

Class	Range of ASVs(cm^3g^{-1})
Sugars	$0.60 - 0.62$
Polyols (from monosaccharides)	$0.65 - 0.68$
Polyols (from disaccharides)	$0.62 - 0.64$
Hydrogenated glucose syrups (lycasins)	$0.61 - 0.62$
Amino acids	$0.50 - 0.90$

(ASVs) of polyols compared to sugars and amino acids. Clearly the polyols exhibit narrow zones of ASVs and it is therefore not surprising that their tastes are so similar to the sugars. Hydrogenated glucose syrups are indistinguishable from the sugars.

The somewhat high apparent specific volumes of the polyols compared to the sugars means that they are less compatible (than sugars) with water structure. This physicochemical property might account for the markedly poor membrane transport capacity of the polyols. They are slowly absorbed from the intestine which means that heavy doses might cause diarrhoea. The same slow membrane absorption characteristic has been implicated in the accumulation of polyols in the lens of the eye during sugar-induced cataract. Structure-activity studies of this important class of sweeteners are currently underway which should help us to understand the uniquely hydrated state of each polyol molecule in solution and its importance in both taste and metabolism.

PREDICTION OF SWEETNESS BY PHYSICOCHEMICAL PROPERTIES

Many attempts have been made to correlate taste properties with various physicochemical properties. The position is complicated by the requirements of polar, hydrophobic and steric parameters for successful elicitation of the sweet response and no totally satisfactory physical model has yet emerged despite mathematical and psychophysical approaches being attempted (18). All previously attempted physical models have relied solely on structure-activity relationships in vacuo and have ignored parameters such as the accessibility of stimulus to receptor and the role of water. Quite the most imaginative model to date has been that of Daniels (18) who has taken account of diffusion of stimulus to receptor, partitioning onto the membrane, orientation (dipole moment), activity (H-bonding), followed by the same factors in reverse as the stimulus molecule is removed and diffuses away from the receptor vicinity. Good correlations between sweetness intensity and physicochemical parameters have been demonstrated (18) utilising some of the solution data already explained in this chapter (9). The possibility of physico-

chemical and even instrumental prediction of taste appears
to be approaching.

CONCLUSION

Physicochemical properties of sweeteners, particularly in
solution, are essential for an understanding of their
applications in food, physiology and medicine. In
particular, sweetener-water interactions underline all
relevant behaviour and can be used to explain the shape,
size and stability of all sweet molecules.

REFERENCES

1. Grenby, T. Progress in Sweeteners, Elsevier AS,London,
   1989, pp 1-374.

2. Franks, F., Water, Royal Soc.Chemistry, London, 1983,
   pp 1-95.

3. Franks, F., Kay, R.L. and Dadok,J. A nuclear magnetic
   resonance study of isomeric pentitols in aqueous and non-
   aqueous solutions. J.Chem.Soc., Faraday Trans.I, 1988,
   84 (8), 2595-2602.

4. Franks, F., Lillford, P.J. and Robinson, G. Isomeric
   equilibria of monosaccharides in solution. J.Chem.Soc.,
   Faraday Trans I, 1989, 85(8)2417-2426.

5. Symonds, M.C.R. Liquid water - the story unfolds. Chem
   Brit, 1989, May, 491-494.

6. Shallenberger, R.S. and Acree, T.E. Molecular theory of
   sweet taste. Nature, 1967, 216, 480-482.

7. Birch, G.G., Structural relationships of sugars to taste.
   Crit. Rev. Food Sci. Nutr., 1976, 8, 57-97.

8. Birch, G.G. and Lee, C.K., Structural functions of taste
   in the sugar series. J.Fd.Sci., 1974, 39, 947-949.

9. Shamil, S., Birch, G.G., Mathlouthi, M. and Clifford,M.N.
   Apparent molar volumes and tastes of molecules with more
   than one sapophore. Chem.Senses, 1987,12,397-409.

10. Shahidi, F. and Farrell, P.G. Partial molar volumes of
    some α-amino carboxylic acids in water. J.Chem.Soc.,
    Faraday Trans I, 1981, 11, 963-968.

11. Egan,H., Kirk, R.S. and Sawyer, R. Pearsons Chemical
    Analysis of Foods, Churchill Livingstone, London, 8th Edn.,
    1981, pp 216.

12. Von Rymon Lipinski, G.W., Acesulfame K: properties, physiology and applications in calorie-reduced and low-calorie products. In Low-Calorie Products, Eds. G.G.Birch and M.G.Lindley, Elsevier AS, London, 1988, pp 101-112.

13. Birch, G.G. and Kemp, S.E. Apparent specific volumes and tastes of amino acids. Chem.Senses, 1989, 14,249-258.

14. Kemp, S.E., Birch, G.G., Portmann, M.O. and Mathlouthi,M. Intrinsic viscosities and apparent specific volumes of amino acids and sugars. 'Effective size' and taste of sapid molecules. J.Sci.Fd.Agric., 1990, 51, 97-107.

15. Birch, G.G. Sweetness and Sweeteners. Endeavour, 1987, 11(1), 21-24.

16. Sicard, P.J. Hydrogentated glucose syrups, sorbitol, mannitol and xylitol. In Nutritive Sweeteners, Eds. G.G.Birch and K.J.Parker, Elsevier AS, London, 1982, pp 145-170.

17. Kearsley, M.W. The rapid determination of dextrose equivalent of glucose syrups. J.Assoc.Publ.Analysts, 1978, 16, 85-88.

18. Daniel, J.R. Sweeteners. Theory and design. In Frontiers in Carbohydrate Research, Eds. R.P.Millane, J.N. Be Miller and R.Chandrasekaran. Elsevier AS, London, 1990, pp 34-65.

METABOLISM AND TOLERANCE OF SUGARLESS SWEETENERS

P. WÜRSCH
Nestlé Research Centre
Nestec Ltd.
Vers-chez-les-Blanc, 1000 Lausanne-26
Switzerland

ABSTRACT

Sugarless sweeteners are represented by two very different groups of products: 1) the bulk sweeteners can replace weight by weight the common dietary sugars in foods but differ nutritionally by their digestion, absorption, metabolism and by their utilization by dental and colonic bacteria; 2) the intense sweeteners are used in very small amounts and therefore their nutritional significance should be very limited.

Introduction

A considerable interest has emerged during the last decade from consumers, industry and nutritionists for energy-controlled and energy reduced foods, particularly because excess energy intake can lead to obesity, a health risk associated with a number of diseases. It may predispose an individual to hyperlipidemia, hypercholesterolemia, diabetes, gallstone, cancer or hypertension.

Apart from fat, sucrose has been accused as source of excessive energy intake. On the other hand, abundant evidence has been accumulated over several decades that sucrose consumption is closely associated with the development of tooth decay [1]. Thus industry has developed a broad range of alternative sweeteners to fulfil the requirement of reduced energy and non cariogenicity. These can be divided into two categories (Table 1),
- the bulk sweeteners
- the intense sweeteners.

TABLE 1
List of sugarless sweeteners

bulk		intense
Fructose	Palatinose	Saccharin
Erythritol	Maltitol	Cyclamate
Xylitol	Palatinit	Aspartame
Sorbitol	Lycasin	Acesulfame-K
Mannitol	Fructo-	Sucralose
	oligosaccharides	Alitame
		Stevioside

The list is limited to the sweeteners allowed in food in at least one country or might get approval in the near future.

These bulk sweeteners differ from the common dietary sugars by the fact that they are poorly metabolized by the bacteria of the dental plaque, and slowly digested or absorbed in the small intestine of mammals. This review will discuss the metabolism of these sugars at different levels of the body with special emphasis on clinical symptoms [2,3]. The metabolism of fructose will also be discussed, because of its use in pure form mainly for dietetic purposes. The metabolism of the intense sweeteners will be briefly covered in relation to toxicological aspects.

Metabolism of the Sugar Substitutes by the Oral Microflora

Dental caries is an infectious bacterial disease of the dental hard tissues, which results from the interaction of four main factors:
- bacteria on the tooth surface
- fermentable, acidogenic substrates
- susceptible dental enamel
- duration of the contact between the substrate and the bacteria

Tooth decay begins with acid demineralization of the outer enamel surface, and if not stopped, continues into the dentine and pulp. Prevention of dental caries is based on suppressing one of the above mentioned factors. All dietary sugars - sucrose, glucose, fructose, lactose and even starch - after hydrolysis are metabolized by the bacteria of the dental plaque and have a nearly equal capacity to produce acid [4].

34

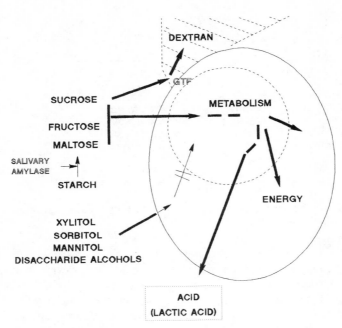

Figure 1. Dietary carbohydrates are a source of energy for the bacteria of the
dental plaque which also produce acid when substrate in excess.
GTF = Glucosyltransferase.

In the presence of a large concentration of substrate, the micro-organisms
must limit the utilization of sugars and thus regulate their metabolism. This is
achieved at three levels, i.e. the transport of the sugar, the glycolytic
pathway, and the conversion of pyruvate into metabolic end-products.

The transport of sugar from the external environment through the cell
membrane into the cytoplasm requires carriers. Streptococci often have two
transport systems for each sugar and three for sucrose [5]. The phosphotransferase system with high affinity for the sugar is induced when the sugar is
present at low concentration, whereas the proton linked active sugar transport
system is used at higher sugar levels. Very little is known about transport
systems for sugar alcohols. Xylitol is transported into the cell of *S.mutans* by
the phosphotransferase system, and xylitol 5-phosphate is accumulated, which
seems to be responsible for the growth inhibition property of xylitol [6].
Maltitol and maltotriitol are very slowly absorbed. The latter inhibits the
transport and phosphorylation of maltose when present concomitantly [7], and
thus limits acid production from maltose [8].

When starving micro-organisms are exposed to an excess of sugar, glycolytic
intermediates might build up in the cell at levels that are even toxic. One way
to defend against this accumulation is to open an alternative metabolic pathway
(lactate gate). The glycolytic intermediates are then rapidly excreted from the

cell, essentially in the form of lactate. High level of metabolizable sugar thus produces a rapid drop of pH and an increase in the concentration of lactate.

Sucrose is the only substrate for the synthesis by *S.mutans* of the sticky dextran, which enable the dental microflora to adhere on the dental surface.

One approach, among others, to reduce dental caries has been to reduce the frequency of contact of sucrose with the dental plaque by substituting sucrose by non metabolizable sweeteners. These sweeteners should then not be useable as a substrate for the synthesis of dental plaque.

Several long term caries studies have convincingly demonstrated that a partial substitution of sugar by non cariogenic alternative sweeteners, in particular xylitol, has beneficial consequences on the dental health [9]. None of the sugar alcohols so far used as sugar substitutes have shown to be metabolized significantly by the dental plaque microflora, and thus produce both *in vitro* and *in vivo* no little or no drop in pH of the dental plaque [10]. However, some recent studies indicate that the oral microflora can adapt to the prolonged exposure of sugar alcohols in the human diet, in particular to sorbitol and sorbitol-containing carbohydrates. This aspect has been extensively reviewed by Linke [11].

Digestion of Di- and Oligosaccharides

The digestion of disaccharides and oligosaccharides is assured by a limited number of enzymes, which are "intrinsic membrane proteins" of the epithelial cells of the brush border of the intestinal mucosa. They are located in close proximity to the active transport site. They are thus freely accessible to their substrate from the lumen. These enzymes are the sucrase-isomaltase complex, glycoamylase and lactase [12].

The sucrase fraction can be defined as an α-glucosidase which has a preference for hydrolysing sucrose(α-1,2linkage), maltose(α-1,4 linkage) and higher oligosaccharides like maltotriose and maltopentaose. This enzyme is able to split maltitol but at a much lower rate than maltose. Isomaltase readily hydrolyzes maltose, maltitol, the α-1,6 linkages of isomaltose, and palatinose [13,14].

Sucrase-isomaltase accounts for 80-90% of the total maltase activity in normal human small intestine. The remaining activity is found in another carbohydrase, glucoamylase, which can also be called oligosaccharidase because, apart from hydrolyzing maltose, it can hydrolyze terminal 1,4 bonds of limit dextrins [15].

Lactase can split a number of β-glycosides, among them lactose, but lactitol at a very low rate and lactulose, not at all. The rate of digestion of lactitol by human intestinal mucose homogenates is reported to be 1-3% of that of lactose which is itself around 25% that of sucrose [16].

Absorption and Intestinal Tolerance of Sugar Substitutes and their Digestion Products.

The common dietary monosaccharides, glucose, galactose and fructose, are exceptionnally well absorbed in the small intestine through special transfer mechanisms of "facilitated diffusion" and of "active transfer". In both cases the hexose is moved across the brush border membrane at a rate faster than can be accounted for by simple diffusion [17]. Simple diffusion and facilitated diffusion both depend on the concentration of the sugar in the intestinal lumen. At lower intestinal concentrations of glucose, its absorption occurs almost exclusively by way of active transfer but when the sugar concentration is correspondingly high, passive transfer can become predominant [18]. The absorption of polyols like sorbitol, mannitol and xylitol takes place exclusively by means of free diffusion, or hypothetically, by transport systems not yet discovered, with a very low affinity for these polyols. Their absorption rate is thus considerably lower than for the common dietary sugars as shown in Figure 2 [19].

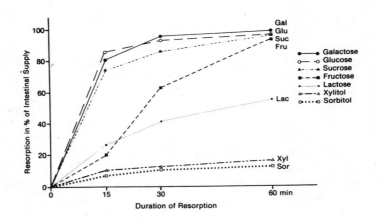

Figure 2. Absorption of 10% solutions of carbohydrate by rats [19].

It is, therefore, hardly possible to induce malabsorption or even diarrhoea in a healthy human subject using rapidly absorbable sugars, glucose or galactose. In the case of fructose, risk of osmotic diarrhoea can occur at relatively high intake [20] but significant malabsorption can occur at lower doses, if glucose is not present at the same time. For sugar alcohols, especially when administered in a solution, the threshold dosage is significantly lower than for fructose, making malabsorption and diarrhoea occur at lower doses.

Osmotic diarrhoea can occur through different phenomena which are related to an excessive amount of low molecular weight substances in the intestine.

First there is a close resemblance between the sugar alcohols and the osmotically active laxatives like Epsom salt (magnesium sulfate), in the way that diarrhoea is induced. This occurs by an accumulation of water in the intestinal region due to an insufficient absorption of sugars in the small intestine when these are administered in relatively high dosages, especially in the isolated form of drinks. Second the unabsorbed fraction reaches the large intestine, and here the laxative effect can be significantly increased through the influence of bacteria.

The catabolic products of sugar fermentation by the bacteria, namely the short chain fatty acids, might increase, or decrease the osmotic effectiveness, depending on the difference between the rate of their production and the rate of acid clearance from the large intestine. These acids are completely ionised at the pH of the large intestine due to their low pKa value. If we assume that one mol of sorbitol will produce 1.4 mol of organic acids, based on the equation of Wolin (chapter 5), which will then bind 1.4 equivalent of cations, the osmotic effect of the sorbitol reaching the large intestine will almost triple. However, the increase in ion concentration will be partially or totally offset by their absorption by the large intestinal mucosa. In the case of lactose intolerance, which occurs in large groups of the world's adult population, 7-14 g of lactose can induce diarrhoea. This pronounced effect of small quantities of the disaccharide is explained by the rather high molecular weight of the sugar and its rapid decomposition in the large intestine. One mole of lactose could yield theoretically 5.6 moles of organic salt.

The tolerance threshold value varies considerably with each individual, partly because of the difference in absorption capacity. Beaugerie [21] found between 7% and 30% malabsorption from 10 g of ingested sorbitol by humans. Undesirable symptoms appeared at 40 g/day of lactitol or sorbitol as shown in Figure 3 [22] and 30 g/day or 25 g single dose of maltitol [23].

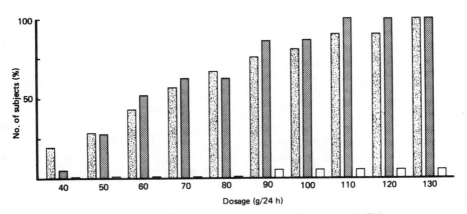

Figure 3. Cumulative frequency of laxative threshold of lactitol (☼), sorbitol (☷) and glucose ( ) in human subjects (n = 21) [22].

Watery diarrhoea occured within one hour in 40% of the subjects who ingested 60 g/day lactitol or sorbitol, or 40 g maltitol. For xylitol, the threshold value at which diarrhoea is induced lies much higher, since most human subjects can tolerate 30 g in a single dose. In the Turku sugar study, xylitol was well tolerated, and in some cases more than 200 g were consumed in one day with only rare cases of laxative symptoms [24]. It is not clear whether this adaptation is caused by an increased absorption of the polyol or by an adaptation of the colonic bacteria to ferment this polyol.

Adaptation in rats has been attributed to an increased rate of xylitol dehydrogenation in the liver and an increased rate of disappearance from the blood, thus lowering the concentration gradient across the intestinal mucosal membrane. However, recently, Krishnan et al [25] reported that adaptation had essentially no effect on the liver homogenate to produce $^{14}CO_2$ from labelled xylitol, and no major changes were found in hepatic enzymes. A more likely explanation of adaptation is that it results from the presence of caecal bacteria that can metabolize xylitol, and which in the continued presence of xylitol, are able to increase this ability several fold. An analogous adaptation has been reported for L-sorbose in humans and rats. At high loads of sorbose, residual sugar was found in the faeces and osmotic diarrhoea occured over a few days. The fermentation adaptation occured fairly rapidly, accompanied by some flatulence [26].

Intestinal Fermentation of Carbohydrate

The bulk of the bacteria of the gastrointestinal tract of humans reside in the large intestine, and the main metabolic functions involve generation of energy, for growth and maintenance from anaerobic degradation of organic matter delivered by the small intestine. Most of the bacteria in the large intestine derive their energy primarily from carbohydrates and their derivatives [27]. Carbohydrates are hydrolyzed and fermented mainly to acetate, propionate, butyrate, CO_2 and H_2 by a complex of fermentative bacteria which are represented by 10^{-11} -10^{12} bacteria/g faeces [28] (Figure 4). The microflora is thus able to utilize only a fraction of the potential energy available for maintenance and growth. These unabsorbed carbohydrates are provided by the diet and from endogenous complex polysaccharides. The Western and Japanese diets provide about 20-25 g dietary fibre and about 5 g are lost in the faeces.

Starch is also a significant source of carbohydrate for the microflora. Recent studies on the digestibility of starch involving ileostomized patients showed that a starch fraction escapes digestion and absorption in the small intestine. The proportion depends very much on the source of starchy food and on the process it underwent. The lowest level, is 0.5% from rice and the highest, white bean with roughly 10% of the digestible starch [29]. The total daily starch malabsorption, including the so-called resistant starch, can be estimated at less than 10 g. This has to be added to 20-25 g of dietary fibre, from which about 5 g are lost in the faeces.

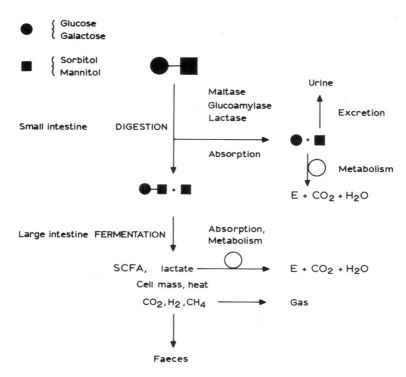

Figure 4. The metabolic fate of disaccharide alcohols [3].

Therefore 20-30 g dietary carbohydrate should be fermented in the large intestine and this figure has to be kept in relation to the extra provision of unabsorbed carbohydrate from sugar substitutes. Besides these carbohydrates, the large intestinal microflora receives also mucins from the desquamation of the small intestine. Several stochiometric equations of fermentation of the large intestine have been proposed, among them, that of Miller and Wolin [27]: 35.5 mol hexose + 48 mol acetate + 11 mol propionate + 5 mol butyrate + 23.7 mol methane + 34.25 mol carbon dioxide. They calculated that the short-chain fatty
acids account for approximately 72% of the energy content of the carbohydrate, excluding the substrate used by the microorganisms for their growth.

Anaerobic fermentation *in-vivo* of [U-14C] sorbose by homogenates of human faeces yielded 64.5% short-chain fatty acids [26]. These short-chain fatty acids are rapidly absorbed by the epithelial cells and metabolized by the host. Radiolabelled acids instilled into the human colon were metabolized to carbon dioxide in the breath within hours [30]. The disappearance patterns of the three labelled acids were similar, although butyric acid was eliminated to a greater extent, probably by the epithelial cells themselves [3].

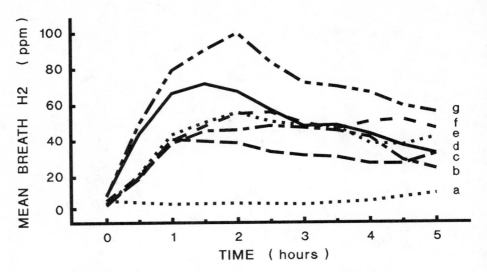

Figure 5. Mean profile of breath hydrogen excretion following ingestion of 10 g hexitol or 19 g disaccharide by seven subjects. Zero hour = initial increase a = basal; b = sorbitol; c = mannitol; d = lactulose; e = palatinit; f = maltitol; g = lactitol [31].

In a majority of humans, colonic bacteria produce very little methane, but rather hydrogen, which can be detected in the breath. Measuring breath hydrogen is the method of choice for detecting carbohydrate malabsorption. Most of the sugar alcohols allowed for consumption are partially malabsorbed as shown in Figure 5. The highest response was observed with lactitol, which is believed to be totally malabsorbed.

Are the malabsorbed sugar substitutes always metabolized by the colonic bacteria? Some rare cases of non fermentation in the colon have been reported, but the phenomenon is only transient as shown with L-sorbose, an epimer of D-fructose. This ketohexose was thought some 12 years ago to be a potential noncariogenic bulk sweetener [32], but it was found to be toxic to dogs [33]. The absorption of this sugar in the small intestine is passive and very slow, and part of it reaches the large intestine. When 14C-sorbose was administered orally to rats, 46% of the radioactivity was recovered intact in the faeces and 16% as carbon dioxide. However, after a few days of adaptation by feeding the rats with sorbose, 6.6% of the radioactivity provided by a single dose of 14C-sorbose, was recovered in the faeces and 59% in carbon dioxide. The radiorespirometric profiles between the unadapted and the adapted rats differ in many respects as shown in Figure 6. In the first situation no fermentation occured and only the absorbed L-sorbose was metabolized. After a few days, all the unabsorbed L-sorbose was metabolized by the faecal flora. An adaptation period was also required for the human intestinal flora [26].

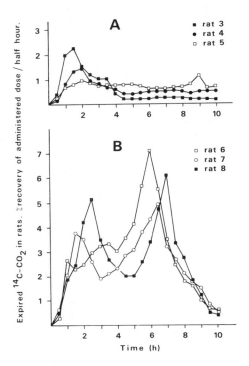

Figure 6. Recovery of $^{14}CO_2$ following a single dose of L-[U-^{14}C]-sorbose to rats before (A) and after adaptation (B) of the intestinal microflora to L-sorbose [26].

However, no adaptation conditions seem necessary for most of the common sugar alcohols [3,23]. Sorbitol is readily fermented in the large intestine, whilst mannitol has been reported to be only partially metabolized [34] and erythritol was fermented after adaptation [35]. The disaccharide alcohols have to be split prior to being metabolized but there is ample bacterial α-glucosidase and β-galactosidase in the large intestine for their hydrolysis. None of these disaccharide alcohols or of their monomer moieties have ever been found in the faeces of humans which suggests that the unabsorbed fractions are completely metabolized by the large intestinal flora.

Energy Value of Sugar Substitutes

The assessment of the energy value of unavailable carbohydrates like dietary fibre is quite difficult because one has to examine the energy balance. The experiment must be carried out in realistic conditions, which means that one will measure very small changes in the metabolizability of a diet. However, it is now generally admitted that the metabolism of the unavailable carbohydrates by the colonic bacteria is profitable for the host, and the efficiency of conversion of food energy into faecal energy is considered to be approximately 30%. An analysis of energy values for unavailable carbohydrates was made, based on 29 human diets, with unavailable carbohydrate ranging from 4 to 94 g/day. For completely fermented polysaccharides, the value was situated around 2.8 kcal/g [36]. In the case of the sugar substitutes, the assessment of available energy is much more difficult and probably varies considerably between individuals, doses of intake, type of sweetener and of food. This is because digestion and absorption are partial in most cases, and thus the amount reaching the large intestine is very variable. Many different methods have been used and which have been described elsewhere with special emphasis on sugar alcohols [3]. Precise values for each individual sweetener or one value for all sweeteners have been proposed by various scientific study groups and particularly the Dutch Nutrition Council [37].

Metabolism of the Sugar Substitutes

Fructose

Fructose is widely distributed in the plant kingdom since it is found in many fruits and berries and even makes-up the majority of the sugar in apples, pears, cherries [38]. Fructose is also one half of the sucrose molecule. The intestinal absorption of fructose is much slower than that of glucose or galactose and it even appears to be incomplete when taken alone [20]. It is absorbed by accumulation against its concentration gradient by an energy- and sodium-dependent process [39]. The absorption of fructose fed in solution appears to be enhanced by the presence of glucose [40]. This would explain why fructose from sucrose, high fructose corn syrup and invert sugar is more readily absorbed. In man fructose enters the portal venous blood largely unchanged.

Fructose has special metabolic features in comparison with glucose: targeting to the liver as the obligatory site of its metabolism, it can cause a great load on this tissue. The ketohexose undergoes phosphorylation to fructose-1-phosphate by a specific fructokinase, which is not dependent on insulin. In doing so, it consumes large amounts of ATP, which is normally regenerated as the fructose-1-phosphate formed is split into glyceraldehyde and dihydroxyacetone phosphate [41]. The metabolism of fructose in man is very rapid, its half-life being approximately 18 minutes [42].

Among positive aspects of fructose is the virtual absence of pancreatic insulin secretion, sparing the B-cells in diabetes and allowing catabolic reactions to proceed e.g adipose tissue lipolysis. This fructose property has a beneficial potential, when used cautiously. However, it must be emphasized that even if diabetics can convert fructose to glucose, tissue utilisation of this latter glucose does require insulin [43].

Chronic consumption of fructose in moderate amounts (60-70 g/day) does not cause significant changes in serum triglyceride or cholesterol levels of healthy humans [44]. However, in subjects with hypertriglyceridemia, consumption of large quantities of fructose can have deleterious effects by increasing the synthesis of triglycerides, but their blood levels tend to return with time to the initial values. In controlled diabetes, acute or a few weeks of moderate consumption of fructose has no adverse effects on the level of blood glucose, cholesterol, and triglycerides [1].

Xylitol

Xylitol is a pentitol which occurs naturally but in small concentrations in many fruits and vegetables and is industrially produced by catalytic hydrogenation of xylose, obtained by the hydrolysis of xylan derived from birchwood chips. Xylitol is also synthesised in the human, mostly in the liver in the range of 5-15 g daily [45]. Xylitol absorption from the intestinal lumen takes place by free diffusion. By this mechanism, resorption is considerably slower and thus affects the intestinal content. Xylitol absorption was measured in healthy subjects using the aspiration technique. Test meals consisted of solutions containing 5 to 20 g of xylitol plus an equal amount of glucose. Mean absorption over the dose range was from 72 to 95% [46]. However, within the range of values reported, absorption did not appear to be dose dependent. Malabsorption of xylitol did not appear to change after ingestion of 30 g xylitol daily for 2-3 weeks. The major part of absorbed xylitol is metabolized in the liver by the widely accepted pathway involving oxidation by iditol dehydrogenase to D-xylulose. The bulk of the xylulose is then phosphorylated by xylulokinase. In turn, it is converted mainly to hexose-6-phosphate intermediate by the enzymes of the pentose shunt pathway, and finally to glucose. It is therefore an effective source of glycogen production [47]. Xylitol is utilized by the liver and to a smaller extent kidney and other tissues, whilst other organs like brain, adipocytes, lungs and muscles cannot metabolize the polyol.

During the Turku diet study the mean daily intake of xylitol was around 50 g, the high range being at 200 - 400 g. Transient osmotic diarrhoea occured at the beginning, but gradually receded [24]. It was possible to administer 30 g of xylitol per day over a period of 4 weeks to diabetic children [48]. The efficacy of xylitol in the prevention of dental caries has been highlighted in the Turku studies. Since then, numerous clinical caries trials have been accomplished which confirmed the early findings [9]. The consumption of small daily quantities of xylitol ranging from 7 to 20 g per subject in the form of chewing gum decreased significantly the incidence of dental caries in children and in adults.

This effect is both dose and concentration dependent and is the result of several complex physico-chemical and metabolic actions [9]. Xylitol interacts with calcium, saliva and plaque fluid and thus contributes to the remineralization of mineral-deficient enamel sites. Xylitol is not metabolized by the mixed plaque flora and no adaptation has been observed. However, strains of S.mutans take up xylitol but cannot metabolize it, and it may inhibit the glycolytic enzymes of the bacteria. Finally it decreases the amount and adhesion of the polysaccharides produced from sucrose.

Sorbitol and mannitol

Sorbitol is slowly absorbed. The proportion absorbed seems to be comparable to that of maltitol and palatinit [3,21,31]. The hexitol is converted in the liver into fructose.

Mannitol is only very partially absorbed in the small intestine and mostly excreted in urine [34]. The unabsorbed fraction of both hexitols undergoes complete fermentation by the coloric flora.

Sorbitol and mannitol are metabolized slowly by only a few of the oral bacterial strains. Therefore the production of acid *in-vitro* and *in-vivo* was found much less than from glucose [11]. However, after several weeks of mouth rinses with sorbitol solutions, the mean acid production from dental plaque suspensions significantly increased, suggesting adaptation of the oral microflora [49].

The disaccharide alcohols

The kinetics of hydrolysis of maltitol, palatinit and lactitol by the intestinal mucose enzyme of mammals has been extensively studied by several groups [2,14,16,54]. Although maltitol and palatinit are slowly hydrolyzed as compared to maltose, they are partially digested *in-vivo* in rats, pigs and humans and part of the disaccharide alcohol and part of released sorbitol and mannitol, the latter from palatinit, reach the large intestine and are fermented [2,21,31,55]. Lactitol digestibility, as already mentioned, is very low and it has been shown to be totally unabsorbed [22].

Erythritol

Erythritol is a rare four carbon polyalcohol, which has a sweetness of about 75% that of sucrose and is formed during fermentation of food. It can be produced in large amounts by fermentation of glucose or sucrose with *Aureobasidium sp.* Glycerol is readily absorbed from the small intestine and metabolized, whereas erythritol is mostly excreted in the urine. When C-erythritol (0.1 g/kg body weight) was administered to humans, 80% of the radioactivity was excreted in urine and 6% only in expired air [35]. At 10 and 20 g dosage, 90% of erythritol was recovered in urine. It was suggested, that a small fraction of the polyalcohol entered the large intestine and was metabolized by the bacteria. The intestinal microflora needed to be adapted in order to metabolize efficiently this polyalcohol, as observed with L-sorbose [26]. The metabolizable energy was estimated at less than 0.4 kcal/g.

Palatinose

Palatinose, α -D-glucopyranosyl-1,6-fructose, chemically named isomaltulose, is industrially produced by enzymatic conversion of sucrose. It is found in small quantity in honey. This reducing disaccharide is hydrolysed by the rat and human intestinal sucrase isomaltase complex [14, 50]. In rat, palatinose is hydrolysed in competition with isomaltose and its hydrolysis is not inhibited by acarbose, which is a specific inhibitor of sucrase [50]. Therefore it looks like the disaccharide is hydrolysed specifically by the isomaltase. This slow digestion rate is responsible for the blunted glycemic and insulinemic responses to a palatinose load as compared to sucrose [51]. No intestinal discomfort has been reported, even at 1 g/kg body weight palatinose, suggesting that the disaccharide was completely digested [51].

The cariogenicity, or more precisely the lack of it, has been reviewed comprehensively by Takazoe [52], by showing that this sugar is not utilized by most strains of Streptococcus mutans . After 6 weeks of daily mouth rinses with palatinose, the human dental plaque, was able to metabolize the sugar which produced a significant drop of the dental plaque pH. Its acid production activity was about one third that from glucose. These results suggest that some adaptation occured probably by an ecological change in the mouth [53].

Caries incidence on rats fed palatinose diet (56%) was low compared to rats on a sucrose diet, and only buccal caries were induced with palatinose. The mean caries score was roughly 5 times lower. The S.mutans E-49 inoculated at the beginning of the study disappeared almost completely under the palatinose diet suggesting that the sugar does not support the growth of at least this strain of S.mutans [52]. Finally no water-insoluble glucan was synthesized from palatinose and its presence had an inhibitory effect on glucan synthesis from sucrose.

Lycasin

Lycasin is a mixture of sorbitol, maltitol, maltotriitol and hydrogenated oligosaccharides. The glucose-glucose bonds of the hydrogenated oligosaccharides are split by α-amylase, yielding mostly maltose, maltitol and maltotriitol. Maltotriitol in turn is rapidly hydrolyzed into maltitol and glucose by the small intestinal glucoamylase [8,54].

Many experiments of acid production of the dental plaque in-vitro and in-vivo have shown that Lycasin 80/55 is slowly fermented and produces a pH drop comparable to maltitol, lactitol and sorbitol [56]. It was suggested, that catabolism by the bacteria of the small amounts of maltose produced by salivary α -amylase is inhibited by maltotriitol present in Lycasin [7,8].

The fructo-oligosaccharides

Fructo-oligosaccharides, 1-(β-fructofuranosyl)n-1-sucrose or inulin occur in many plants, in particular artichoke and chicory, but due to their rather high molecular size, they are categorized as soluble fibre. However, oligosaccharides with short chain length have been biosynthesized, by transferring fructose to a sucrose acceptor. The mixture, named Neosugar[R], contains 1-kestose (GF_2), nystose (GF_3), fructosyl-nystose (GF_4) and trace of sucrose. Other approaches consist of partially hydrolysing inulin, or selecting plant varieties which produce only short chain oligomers. These oligosaccharides are not hydrolysed by the enzymes of the intestinal mucosa [57], but totally fermented by the large intestinal microflora. The radiorespirometric pattern, obtained in a human subject who consumed

[^{14}C]fructo-oligosaccharides, showed a progressive increase rate of $^{14}CO_2$ expiration with a maximum at around 7 hours, suggesting that negligible amount of the carbohydrate was metabolized by the host. The recovery of radioactivity in the faeces was 10%. The radiolabelled fructo-oligosaccharides incubated in human faeces, in anaerobic conditions, were rapidly catabolized with incorporation of 58% of radioactivity in short chain fatty acids [58]. The fructo-oligosaccharides are claimed to be selectively utilized by the intestinal bacteria and thus promote the growth of the bifidobacteria [59]. After 2 weeks of consumption of 8 g/day Neosugar^R, a mean ten fold increase of bifidobacteria was observed, without any change in the total bacterial count. The increase was particularly high in subjects who had a rather low count of bifidobacteria. However, the number of subjects tested was rather small. One of the fructo-oligosaccharides, nystose, has been shown to be anaerobically metabolized by pooled samples of dental plaque at a rate similar to that of Lycasin, suggesting that its cariogenic potential might be significant. The sugar, however, is not a substrate for glucosyl-transferase, the dental plaque forming enzyme [57].

Metabolism of the Intense Sweeteners

Saccharin, Cyclamate, Acesulfame-K, Sucralose

These molecules, completely synthetic, are not metabolized in mammals and excretion takes place mainly in the urine.

Aspartame

It is a dipeptide methyl ester (L-aspartyl-L-phenylalanine-methyl ester) consisting of two amino acids. It is hydrolysed in the small intestine at the mucosal surface by dipeptidases, absorbed and rapidly metabolized in humans. Aspartic acid is metabolized into carbon dioxide whereas phenylalanine is primarily incorporated into body protein [60].

Phenylalanine is an essential amino acid. Sustained levels of this amino acid in the blood and body tissues can cause permanent brain damage. However, in normal humans, the toxic levels of phenylalanine in the blood did not occur in a test in which an equivalent of 600 sweetener tablets were consumed. In fact a heavy use of aspartame-sweetened products would increase the daily phenylalanine consumption by about 6%. There was however much concern for people who have the hereditary disease phenylketonuria. They cannot consume diet that contains normal amounts of phenylalanine, but many studies have shown, that even phenylalanine from an abuse dose of aspartame is adequately but slowly metabolized and cleared [61]. In the case of aspartic acid, no signifiant change in blood level was observed with high load of aspartic acid even with concomitant consumption of glutamic acid, which can easily be converted into aspartic acid in the body.

Methanol seemed to have aroused the greatest public concern, but there is no scientific evidence that the consumption of methanol in the amounts present in aspartame-sweetened products might pose a health hazard. Methanol is oxidized in the one-carbon metabolic pool to carbon dioxide. At 200 mg/kg dose, no increase in formate, an intermediate toxic metabolite, could be detected in the blood [62].

Alitame

Alitame is formed from L-aspartic acid, D-alanine and a novel thietanyl amine. Alitame is well absorbed in the small intestine after hydrolysis of the peptide bond. Most of the oral dose is excreted in urine in the form of conjugated and/or oxidized sulphur of the amide fragment.
The remainder is excreted in faeces, mainly as unchanged alitame. The aspartic acid fraction is absorbed and metabolized.

Stevioside

This diterpenglycoside is extracted from Stevia Rebaudiana bertoni and is characterized by an intense sweetness. The substance is not absorbed in the small intestine, but degraded to the diterpenoid aglycone, steviol, by rat intestinal microflora. This is then absorbed and excreted in bile [63].

Conclusion

The perfect low-calorie sweetener would substitute zero or nearly zero calorie for the caloric value, and bulk of the replaced carbohydrate. However, none of these sugarless sweeteners so far fulfill alone these requirements: either they provide bulk, and sweetness but also significant energy to the body, or they have a very intense sweetness and thus do not provide bulk and energy. Nevertheless most of the bulk sweeteners should contribute to dental caries prevention and have a reduced energy value, but the nutritional significance of this last point can be disputed in regard of the low acceptable daily intake.

REFERENCES

1. Glinsmann, W.H., Irausquin, H. and Park, Y.K., Evaluation of health aspects of sugars contained in carbohydrate sweeteners. Report of Sugars Task Force, FDA, 1986.

2. Ziesenitz, S.C. and Siebert, G., The metabolism and utilization of polyols and other bulk sweeteners compared with sugar. In Development in sweeteners, ed. T.H. Grenby, Elsevier Applied Science Pub. Ltd., Barking, UK, 1987, 3, pp. 109-149.

3. Würsch, P. and Anantharaman, G., Aspects of the energy value assessment of the polyols. In Progress in Sweeteners, ed. T.H. Grenby, Elsevier Science Pub., 1989, pp. 241-266.

4. Mörmann, J.E. Mühlemann, H.R., Oral starch degradation and its influence on acid production in human dental plaque. Caries Res., 1981, 15, 166-175.

5. Slee, A.M. and Tanzer, J.M., Sucrose transport by *Streptococcus mutans*. Evidence for multiple transport systems. Biochim.Biophys. Acta, 1982, **692**, 415-424.

6. Reiner, A.M., Xylitol and d-arabitol toxicities due to derepressed fructose, galactitol, and sorbitol phosphotransferase of *E.coli*, J. Bact., 1977, **132**, 166-173.

7. Würsch, P. and Koellreutter, B., Maltotriitol inhibition of maltose metabolism in *S.mutans* via maltose transport, amylomaltase and phospho-α-glucosidase activities. Caries Res., 1985, **19**, 439-449.

8. Würsch, P. and Koellreutter, B., Maltitol and maltotriitol as inhibitor of acid production in human dental plaque. Caries Res., 1982, **16**, 90-95.

9. Mäkinen, K.K., Latest dental studies on xylitol and mechanism of action of xylitol in caries limitation. In Progress in sweeteners, ed. T.H. Grenby, Elsevier Applied Science, 1989, pp. 331-362.

10. Imfeld, T., Evaluation of the cariogenicity of confectionary by intra-oral wire telemetry, Schweiz. Mschr. Zahnheilk., 1977, **87**, 437-464.

11. Linke, H.A.B., Sweeteners and dental health in the influence of sugar substitutes on oral microorganisms. In Developments in sweeteners, ed. T.H. Grenby, Elsevier Applied Science Pub. Ltd., Barking, UK, 1987, **3**, pp. 151-188.

12. Semenza, G., Intestinal oligo-and disaccharides. Carbohydrate metabolism and its disorders. In Randel, Steiner, Whelan, Academic Press, London, 1981, **3**, pp. 425-479.

13. Cogoli, A., Mosimann, H., Vock, C., Von Balthazar, A.K. and Semenza, G., A simplified procedure for the isolation of the sucrase-isomaltase complex from rabbit intestine. Eur.J.Biochem., 1972, **30**, 7-14.

14. Ziesenitz, S.C., Carbohydrasen aus jejunalmucosa des Menschen. Z.Ernährungswiss., 1986, **25**, 253-258.

15. Taravel, F., Datema, R., Woloszczuk, W., Marshall, J.J. and Whelan, W.J., Purification and characterization of a pig intestinal α-limit dextrinase. Eur.J.Biochem., 1983, **130**, 147-153.

16. Nilsson, U. and Jägerstad, M., Hydrolysis of lactitol, maltitol and Palatinit by human intestinal biopsies. Br.J.Nutr., 1987, **58**, 199-206. 17. Kimmich, G.A., Intestinal absorption of sugar. In Physiology of the gastrointestinal tract, ed. L.R. Johnson, Raven Press, 1981, pp. 1035-1061.

17. Macrae, A.E., Neudoerffer, T.A., Support for the existence of an active transport mechanism of fructose in the rat. Biochem.Biophys.Acta., 1972, **288**, 137-144.

18. Murakami, E., Saito, M. and Suda, M., Contribution of diffusive pathway in intestinal absorption of glucose in rat under normal feeding conditions. Experientia 1977, **33**, 1469-1470.

19. Mehnert, H. and Förster, H., Study of the evacuation mechanism of the stomach after oral administration of different sugars in man and rat. Diabetologia, 1968, **4**, 26-33.

20. Ravich, W.J., Bayless, T.M. and Thomas, M., Fructose: incomplete intestinal absorption in humans. Gastroenterology, 1983, **84**, 26-29.

21. Beaugerie, L., Contribution à l'étude du transport intestinal du sorbitol chez l'homme. Thesis, Hôpital St. Lazare, Paris, 1987.

22. Dharmaraj, H., Patil, H., Grimble, G.K. and Silk, D.B.A., Lactitol, a new hydrogenated lactose derivative: intestinal absorption and laxative threshold in normal human subjects. Brit.J.Nutr., 1987, **57**, 195-199.

23. Abraham, R.R., Davis, M., Yudkin, J. and Williams, R., Controlled clinical trial of a new non-calorigenic sweetening agent. J.Human Nutrition, 1981, **35**, 165-172.

24. Mäkinen, K.K. and Scheinin, A., Turku sugar study. VI. The administration of the trial and the control of the dietary regimen. Acta Odont.Scand., 1975, **33** (suppl. 70), 105-127.

25. Krishnan, R. and James, H.M. et al, Some biochemical studies on the adaptation associated with xylitol ingestion in rats. Aust.J.Exp.Biol.Med.Sci., 1980, **58**, 627-638.

26. Würsch, P., Welsch, C. and Arnaud, M.J., Metabolism of L-Sorbose in the rat and the effect of the intestinal microflora on its utilisation both in the rat and in the human. Nutr.Metab., 1979, **23**, 145-155.

27. Miller, T.L. and Wolin, M.J., Fermentation by saccharolytic intestinal bacteria. Am.J.Clin.Nutr., 1979, **32**, 164-172.

28. Moore, W.E.C., Cato, E.P. and Holderman, L.U., Some current concepts in intestinal bacteriology, Am.J.Clin.Nutr., 1978, **31**, S33-S42.

29. Würsch, P., Starch in human nutrition. Wrld Rev.Nutr.Diet, 1989, **60**, 199-256.

30. Høverstadt, T., Bøhmer, T. and Fausa, O., Absorption of short-chain fatty acids from the human colon measured by the [14]C0 breath test. Scand.J.Gastroenterol., 1982, **17**, 373-378.

31. Würsch, P., Koellreutter, B. and Schweizer, T., Hydrogen excretion after ingestion of five different sugar alcohols and lactulose. Eur.J.Clin.Nutr., 1989, **43**, 819-825.

32. Mühlemann, H.R. and Schneider, P., The effect of sorbose on pH of mixed saliva and interproximal plaque. Helv.Odont.Acta, 1976, **19**, 76-80.

33. Keller, P. and Kistler, A., The haemolytic effect of sorbose in dogs. Experientia, 1977, **33**, 1380-1382.

34. Nasrallah, S.M. and Iber, F.L., Mannitol absorption and metabolism in man. Am.J.Med.Sci., 1969, **258**, 80-88.

35. Oku, T. and Noda, K. The erythritol balance study and evaluation of its metabolizable energy. Intern. Symp. "Caloric evaluation of carbohydrate", Kyoto, Jan. 11-12, 1990.

36. Livesey, G., Energy values of unavailable carbohydrate and diets: An inquiry and analysis. Am.J.Clin.Nutr. 1990, **51**, 617-637.

37. Dutch Nutrition Council. The energy value of sugar alcohols. Voedingsraad, The Hague, 1987.

38. Trautner, K. and Somogyi, J.C., Zuckergehalte von Obst und Gemüse. Einflüsse von Reifegrad, Sorte und Lagerung. Mitt. Gebiete Lebensm. Hyg. 1979, **70**, 497-508.

39. Macrae, A.R. and Neudoerffer, T.A., Support for the existence of an active transport mechanism of fructose in the rat. Biochim.Biophys. Acta, 1972, **288**, 137-144.

40. Rumessen, J.J. and Gudmand-Høyer, E., Absorption capacity of fructose in healthy adults. Comparison with sucrose and its constituent monosaccharides. Gut, 1986, **27**, 1161-1168.

41. Miller, M., Craig, J.W., Drucker, W.R. and Woodward, H., The metabolism of fructose in man. Yale J.Biol.Med., 1956, **29**, 335-360.

42. Froesch, E.A., Fructose metabolism in adipose tissues. Acta Med.Scand.Suppl., 1972, **542**, 37-46.

43. Koivisto, U.A., Fructose as a dietary sweetener in diabetes mellitus. Diabetes Care, 1978, **1**, 241-246.

44. Huttunen, T.K. and Mäkinen, K., Scheinin, A., Turku sugar studies., XI. Effects of sucrose, fructose and xylitol on glucose lipid and urate metabolism. Acta Odontol.Scand., 1975, **33** (supp. 70), 239-245.

45. Hollman, S., Touster, O., Non glycolytic pathways of the metabolism of glucose. Adacemic Press, New York, 1964.

46. Asano, T., Levitt, M.D. and Goetz, F.C., Xylitol absorption in healthy men. Diabetes, 1973, **22**, 279-281.

47. McCormick, D.B. and Touster, O., Conversion of D-[1- C] arabitol, to liver glycogen in the rat and guinea-pig. Biochem.Biophys.Acta, 1961, **54**, 598-600.

48. Förster, H., Boecker, S. and Walther, A., Verwendung von Xylit als Zuckeraustauschstoff bei diabetischen Kindern. Forschr.Med. 1977, **95**, 99-102.

49. Banoczy, J., Hadas, E., Esztari, I., Dreijährige Erfahrungen mit Sorbit im klinischen Längsschnitt-Versuch. Kariesprophylaxe, 1980, **2**, 39-46.

50. Goda, T. and Hosoya, N., Hydrolysis of palatinose by rat intestinal sucrase-isomaltase complex. J.Jap.Soc.Nutr. Food Sci., 1983, **36**, 169-173.

51. Macdonald, I., David, J.W., The bio-availability of isomaltulose in man and rat. Nutr.Rep.Int., 1983, 28, 1083-1090.

52. Kawai, K., Okuda, Y. and Yamashita, K., Changes in blood glucose and insulin after an oral palatinose administration in normal subjects. Endocrinol.Japan., 1985, 32, 933-936.

52. Takazoe, I., Palatinose - an isomeric alternative to sucrose. In Progress in sweeteners, ed. T.H. Grenby, Elsevier Applied Science, 1989, pp. 134-167.

53. Topitsoglou, V., Sasaki, N., Takozoe, I. and Frostell, G., Effect of frequent rinses with isomaltulose (palatinose) solution on acid production in human dental plaque. Caries Res., 1984, 18, 47-51.

54. Würsch, P., Del Vedovo, S., Inhibition of human digestive enzymes by hydrogenated malto-oligosaccharides. Internat.J.Vit.Nutr.Res., 1981, 51, 161-165.

55. Würsch, P., Koellreutter, B., Gétaz, F., Arnaud, M., Metabolism of ^{14}C-maltitol in rats, mice and germ-free mice and comparative digestibility between maltitol and sorbitol in germ-free mice. Br.J.Nutr., 1990, 63, 7-15.

56. Rugg-Gunn, A.J., Lycasin and prevention of dental caries., In Progress in sweeteners, ed. T.H. Grenby, Elsevier Science Pub., 1989, pp. 311-329.

57. Ziesenitz, S.C., Siebert, G., in vitro assessment of Nystose as a sugar substitute. J.Nutr., 1987, 117, 846-851.

58. Hosoya, N., Dhorranintra, B., Hidaka, H., Utilisation of [U-^{14}C]fructooligosaccharides in man as energy resources. J.Clin.Biochem.Nutr., 1988, 5, 67-74.

59. Hidaka, H., Eida, T., Takizawa, T., Tokumaga, T., Tashiso, Y., Effects of fructooligosaccharides on intestinal flora and human health. Bibidobacteria Microflora, 1986, 5, 37-50.

60. Ranney, R.E. , Oppermann, J.A., Muldoon, E., Comparative metabolism of aspartame in experimental animals and humans. Toxicol.Environ.Health, 1976, 2, 441-451.

61. Stegink, L.D., Filer, L.J., Baker, G.L., McDonnell, J.E., Effect of an abuse dose of aspartame upon plasma and erythrocyte levels of amino acids in phenylketonuric heterozygous and normal adults, J.Nutr., 1980, 110, 2216-2224.

62. Stegink, L.D., Brummel, M.C. et al, Blood methanol concentrations in normal adult subjects administered abuse doses of aspartame., J.Toxicol.Environ. Health, 1981, 7, 281-290.

63. Nakayama, K., Kasahara, D., Yamamoto, F., Absorption, distribution, metabolism and excretion of stevioside in rats. J.Food Hygenic. Soc.Jap., 1986, 27, 1-8.

SUGARS, FAT AND DIETARY COUNSELLING

ALISON E. BLACK
Research Dietitian
Dunn Clinical Nutrition Centre,
100 Tennis Court Road, Cambridge, CB2 1QL, UK.

Dentists wish to see a reduction in dietary sugar. Cardiologists however wish for a reduction in dietary fat, and gastroenterologists are focussed on dietary fibre. Sugar is only part of the diet and, if you alter one component, you inevitably alter the balance of all other components. In this paper I consider the place of sugar in the diet as a whole. How does altering sugar intake alter nutrient intake? If sugar comes out of the diet, what will replace it? What is the nutritionally desirable replacement? What is the socially probable replacement?

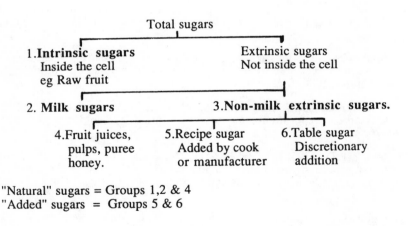

"Natural" sugars = Groups 1,2 & 4
"Added" sugars = Groups 5 & 6

Figure 1.Classification of dietary sugars [1]

Figure 1 shows the classification of sugars devised by the COMA panel [1]. It reflects a certain dietetic pragmatism and an attempt to get away from the terminology of "added" and "natural" sugars. The sugars in whole fruit and in dairy products were deemed not to be as cariogenic as in other foods and were given their own separate groups. All sugars that are "free" in foods, whatever their source, were deemed equally cariogenic and classified under the rather clumsy term Non-Milk Extrinsic Sugars. This includes the sugars in certain foods, namely fruit juices and honey, seen by the general public as "natural" and therefore "good". Sugar in a recipe is no different whether it is put there by a food manufacturer or the housewife.

In this paper I use the terms "total sugars" and, for convenience, "added sugars" rather than Non-Milk Extrinsic Sugars.

Sugars Consumption

Peak consumption of sugar (sucrose + gluscose + honey) was highest in the period 1960 to 1974 with some fluctuations in the years between. Gross supplies available for consumption stood at 143 grams per head per day (17.8 percent of food energy) in 1960 and 142 grams per head per day (16.7 per cent of food energy) in 1974 [1]. Since 1974 there has been a drop in gross supplies and they currently stand at 124 g per head per day (15.7 per cent of energy).

These are the supplies going into the food manufacturing and pharmaceutical industries and into the catering and retail outlets. There are, of course, losses along the chain. If we deduct a figure of 10 percent for losses in the industrial sector, taken from figures obtained by the Monopolies and Mergers Commission 1981, and a further 10 percent for losses in the retail and domestic sectors, the figure used by Ministry of Agriculture Fisheries and Food in estimating household consumption, we obtain an estimated intake of 100 grams per head per day. These constitute the "added augars".

The next level of information on consumption is provided by the National Food Survey. This is an annual survey of about 7000 randomly selected households. During one week each household records all the foods purchased for consumption in the home. Alcoholic drinks and confectionery have always been excluded because they are so often purchased without the knowledge of the person keeping the records. Soft drinks and meals taken outside the home are also left out. The survey therefore has limitations which are particularly important when considering sugars intake.

However in the report of the National Food Survey Committee for 1988 [2] estimates for sugars in alcoholic drinks and confectionery have been obtained from Customs and Excise and trade statistics and added to the household purchases. The report estimated the intake of total sugars at 99 grams per head per day, of which approximately 72 grams came from added sugars. The gap of 30 percent between gross supplies of added sugars and intake measured at the point of consumption is well known. It applies to foods other than sugar and has never been fully explained.

The National Food Survey cannot tell us how intake varies across the age groups and within families. This is of course a question that concerns dentists. The answers would be expected to come from dietary assessments made on individuals. The classic weighed diet record conducted over several days ought in theory to provide a true and complete measure of food intake. However there are a number of problems associated with the assessment of sugars intake by dietary records.

First, the secular trend of falling sugar consumption makes comparisons between surveys invalid if they have been conducted at different periods of time.

Second, there is confusion over the calculating and reporting of sugars intakes. They have been variously reported as total sugars, added sugars (calculated in different ways by different authors) or table sugar only. Sometimes the terms "sugar" or "sugars" have been used without qualification and it is not always clear what is meant.

Third, the very wide range of sugars intakes by individuals and the relatively small numbers studied in many dietary surveys mean that the confidence limits on the measurement of group mean intakes are wide and comparisons between surveys are often on shaky ground.

Figure 2A shows the distribution of total sugars intakes by 405 children in Northumberland studied by Rugg-Gunn, Hackett and colleagues [3,4], and that of 112 women in Cambridge studied by Nelson [5]. There is a 10-20 fold range of intakes from 10-20 grams to over 200 grams; this contrasts with a 4-fold range in energy intakes of the women. Other studies of schoolchildren show similar ranges, and even intakes of pre-school children range from 10-130 grams.

Figure 2B shows the distribution of intakes for Cambridge men [5] superimposed on the curve for children. The range for adult men is even wider and skewed to the right with a tail of very high intakes.

The fourth problem lies with the probability that dietary surveys under-estimate food intake. This conclusion rests on considerations of energy physiology. FAO/WHO/UNU [6] expressed the energy requirements of individuals in terms of multiples of Basal Metabolic

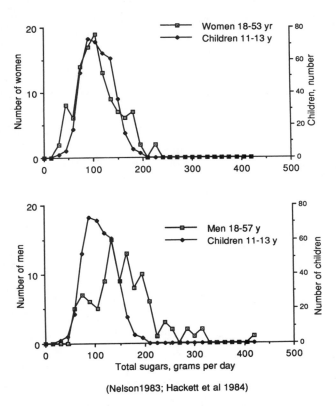

(Nelson1983; Hackett et al 1984)

Figure 2. Distribution of total sugars intakes.

Rate. The average energy requirement for a sedentary lifestyle is given as 1.55 x BMR. This figure is supported by more recent data from whole body calorimetry studies in several countries and from studies of total energy expenditure in free-living conditions using the doubly-labelled water technique (Goldberg et al, in preparation). Since most dietary surveys include measurements of height and weight, it is possible to calculate mean BMR using equations [7] and to relate this to the reported mean energy intake. Examination of published studies shows that in very few does the reported energy intake reach or exceed 1.55 x BMR (Black et al, in preparation). Our knowledge of the size and sources of errors is scanty and at the present time we can only take data at face value while maintaining a critical awareness of possible misinterpretations.

Sugars Consumption in different Age-Sex Groups.

The COMA [1] report tabulated sugars consumption as measured by UK dietary surveys. In spite of the twenty year period covered by the studies, it is difficult to confirm the known secular trend, which is overlaid or obscured by the differences of sample size, sample selection, and the regional and income group differences in intake.

Table 1 shows the mean percent energy from total and added sugars calculated from four studies of pre-school children, five of school children and eleven of adults. Since absolute sugars intake are related to the total amount of food eaten, comparisons between groups are most easily made in terms of the percent of total energy derived from sugars.

TABLE 1.
Mean sugars intake calculated from dietary surveys.
(per cent of energy intake)

	Total sugars	Added sugars
Pre-school children	27.3	16.3
School children	21.4	16.2
Adult men	18.9	13.8
Adult women	19.1	11.1
Dietitians,women	19.3	8.9
Unemployed, Dublin, male	28.4	-
Unemployed, Dublin, female	25.1	-

Pre-school children apparently have a higher total sugars intake than do school children due to a higher intake of dairy products. There seems to be little difference between pre-school and school children in added sugars intake. Children seem to take proportionately more sugars than adults. Women report a lower intake of added sugars than do men, but very similar intakes of total sugars due to their higher consumption of fruit.

Three studies were excluded from the calculation of the adult means. Gibney & Lee [8] studied adults in an area of Dublin with extremely high unemployment. They reported intakes of total sugars which were particularly high due to table sugar taken in many cups of tea. Two studies of dietitians [9,10] showed lower intakes of added sugars than other studies of adult women but without a concomitant reduction in total sugars. This was due to exceptionally high intakes of fruit. These three studies show that a figure for total sugars intake does not of itself adequately categorise the sugars quality of the diet.

The effect of sugar on the nutrient content of the diet.

For the examination of the role of sugar in the diet as a whole, I have used the data of Nelson [5] from a study in 1977/79 of 217 adults in Cambridge. The reported energy intakes are closer to the figure of 1.55 x BMR than in many other studies, and in 1977/79 sugar intakes were higher than at present giving a greater possibility of identifying the effect on nutrient quality.

Dietitians have a particular concept of sugar as "empty" calories ie providing energy but no vitamins. Several authors [3,11,] have shown that high sugars consumers do have lower levels of vitamins and minerals in their diets when expressed per unit of energy. However, these authors also showed that high sugars consumers have higher energy intakes ie they eat more food. The question then becomes, does the larger quantity of food eaten compensate for the lower content of vitamins and minerals such that absolute intakes of nutrients are not compromised.

To examine this question I have first divided the subjects into thirds of the distribution for energy and then subdivided each group into high and low sugars consumers using added sugars intake expressed as the percent of total energy derived from added sugars. The energy and added sugars intake of these groups is shown in Table 2.

TABLE 2.
Energy and added sugars intake in Cambridge adults.

Energy level	High		Middle		Low	
Sugars level	Low	High	Low	High	Low	High
MEN (n=105)						
Energy, kcal	3260	3625	2656	2690	2155	2180
Sugars, % energy	10.8	18.6	10.0	19.7	7.2	18.0
WOMEN (n=112)						
Energy, kcal	2337	2507	1953	1934	1515	1433
Sugars, % energy	8.5	16.3	8.1	15.5	5.1	17.0

Table 3 shows the micronurient intake of each of the six groups of women and of men. Five nutrients have been chosen to represent the quality of the diet. Intakes are expressed as a percentage of the Recommended Daily Allowance so that all are on the same basis and can be compared.

In general within each energy grouping, the low sugars consumers have a higher intake than the high sugars consumers. Thus, when compared on an equal energy basis, sugar has the expected diluting effect on nutrient density. However, in only 5 out of the 30 pairs is the difference statistically significant. In only one pair does the higher sugars intake *per se* push intake below the RDA.

TABLE 3.
Micronutrient intakes in Cambridge adults expressed as a percent of the Recommended Daily Allowance.

Energy level	High		Middle		Low	
Sugars level	Low	High	Low	High	Low	High
MEN (n=105)						
Zinc	91	86	75	69	65	58
Magnesium	109	115	96	88	77	75
Iron	164	165	141	121	115	108
Thiamin	186	130	113	113	104	89
Calcium	278	262	228	231	169	164
WOMEN (n=112)						
Zinc	67	60	55	51	51	41*
Magnesium	82	96	71	71	69	55*
Iron	107	97	88	77*	69	55*
Thiamin	131	122	113	117	92	82
Calcium	216	216	197	176*	148	118

* = p<0 05

If intakes at different energy levels are compared, all high energy groups have a higher intake of micronutrients than any of the middle energy groups. Similarly middle energy groups have higher intakes of micronutrients than do low energy groups. In other words, *the most important determinant of total nutrient intake is total food intake*.

My practical interpretation is that the empty calories effect of sucrose is not as great as is often thought. For individuals with a low energy need (those on reducing diets or with poor appetites), it makes sense to maximise nutrient intake and so to exclude or limit high sugar foods. But for individuals with a high energy requirement, the empty calories effect is probably irrelevant.

The level of sugar in the diet must also affect the balance of the macronutrients. If you alter the intake of one component, then the proportion of all the others will inevitably change. Table 4 shows the percent of energy coming fom each of the macronutrients.

The added sugars intake shows the differences set up by the analysis. There are however only small differences in the starch intakes across all six groups. Starch does seem to be the least variable component of the diet. Total carbohydrate intakes reflect differences in added

TABLE 4

Percent of energy from macronutrients in Cambridge adults.

Energy level	High		Middle		Low	
Sugars level	Low	High	Low	High	Low	High
MEN (n=105)						
Added sugars	10.8	18.6[+++]	10.0	19.7[+++]	7.2	18.0[+++]
Starch	22.8	22.4[ns]	25.2	22.3[ns]	26.5	24.4[ns]
Total CHO	39.4	46.3[+++]	41.5	48.8[+++]	39.7	48.0[+++]
Fat	42.0	37.3[+]	40.7	36.9[+]	41.8	36.8[+++]
Protein	13.0	11.5[+++]	13.0	12.3[ns]	14.5	12.8[+++]
WOMEN (n=112)						
Added sugars	8.5	16.3[+++]	8.1	15.5[+++]	5.1	17.0[+++]
Starch	23.6	23.6[ns]	23.4	24.0[ns]	22.8	23.0[ns]
Total CHO	40.7	47.5[+++]	40.1	47.1[+++]	36.9	46.3[+++]
Fat	42.5	39.6[+]	43.2	38.7[+++]	44.9	38.5[+++]
Protein	13.3	11.6[++]	14.0	13.0[ns]	15.6	13.6[+]

+++=p<0.001, ++=p<0.01, +=p<0.05, ns=not significant

sugars. Fat intakes on the other hand show a pattern that is the inverse of total carbohydrate or added sugars. A lower sugars intake means a higher fat intake and vice versa. This same pattern is seen in other bodies of data. Table 5 shows the findings of Gibney et al [12] in Kilkenny.

TABLE 5.

Percent of energy from macronutrients in 60 Kilkenny adults [12].

Fat level	Low	Moderate	High
% energy from			
Fat	33.0	38.0	49.8
Sucrose	19.1	18.1	12.6

When dietary guidelines were first published several authors turned to their existing data and tried to pull out individuals whose diets already conformed to the guidelines and so identify the characteristics of a healthy eating pattern. All had difficulty in finding individuals with both low fat and low sugar intakes [9,10,12,13]. In a recent paper Cade & Booth [14] report that out of 2340 1-day records only 28 conformed to multiple dietary guidelines and only one of these conformed to both the fat and sugar guidelines.

This must give pause to think. The dietary guidelines for fat are expressed in terms of percent fat energy. If the effect of cutting sugar out of the diet is to raise fat level, then we have to decide which is the more important change to achieve. This point will be discussed again under dietary counselling.

Sources of sugar in the diet.

Figure 3 shows the food sources of sugars in Northumberland children separated into "added" and "natural" sugars [4]. The largest contribution to added sugars was from confectionery, closely followed by table sugar and soft drinks. Cakes, biscuits and puddings added together made a contribution almost equal to that of table sugar. Two categories that many consider undesirably high sources, namely, jams and breakfast cereals, made only a small contribution to sugars intake.

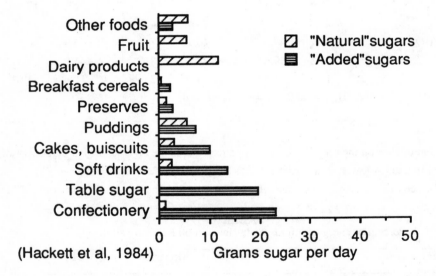

Figure 3. Sources of added and natural sugars in the diet of Northumberland children.

Meat, fish, eggs and vegetables are not shown as they contribute almost no sugar to the diet as calculated by the current food tables. In practice there will be a contribution from the small levels of sugar present in savoury manufactured products. Compared with the quantities coming from the food groups shown, this contribution is likely to be unimportant.

The so-called natural sugars are found in milk and fruit. They are also seen here in puddings which in this analysis included fruit pies, milk pudddings and yoghurts. Since all

61

sugars in all foods except milk and fruit are likely to be equally cariogenic, the following figures show intakes from different food groups only as total sugars. The food groups have also been condensed by putting cakes, biscuits and puddings together, and including preserves with table sugar.

Figure 4 shows the total sugars intake of men and women in Cambridge [5] at the same period of time. Confectionery, was eaten to a much lesser extent by adults. Table sugar was the most important source of sugar for the adults and particularly for the men. The proportion from soft drinks was less important than for children, but the men obtained a significant amount from alcohlic drinks.

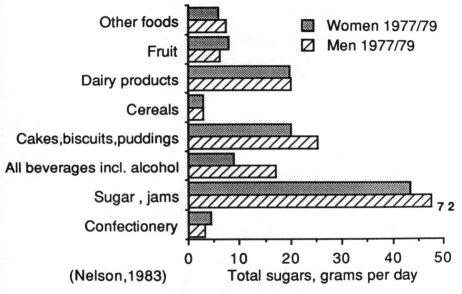

Figure 4. Total sugars intake by food groups, adults 1977/79.

These two surveys were conducted in the late 1970s. In the light of the secular trend for falling sugar consumption we need to ask whether there have been any changes in the sources of sugars.

Figure 5 shows the intake of the Northumberland children compared with a recent study of a similar age group in Belfast (Livingstone, personal communication). The comparison is on shaky ground as the methodologies were different and the numbers in Belfast were very small indeed, only 12 individuals. One difference however stands out strongly and that is the change in soft drink consumption. The survey thus has reflected the known rise in soft drink consumption. The relative importance of the four main sugar providing food groups may have changed. This is shown also in the other age groups studied in Belfast (shown in Figure 6).

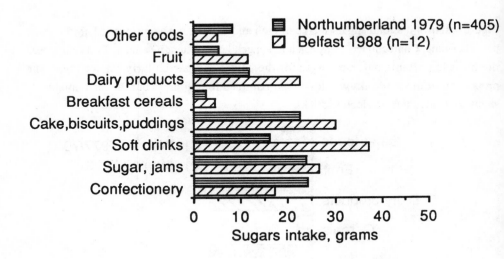

Figure 5. Total sugars intake by food groups, children 11-13 years, 1979 and 1988.

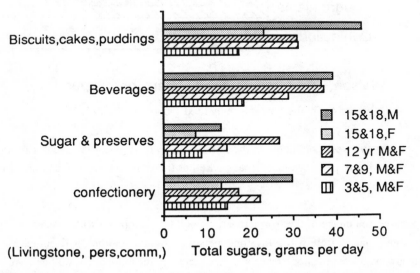

Figure 6. Total sugars intake by food groups of Belfast children of different ages in 1988.

Figure 6 shows the importance of soft drinks, particularly for the teenagers, and the lesser importance of confectionery and of sugar as such. Adolescent boys and girls seem to drink similar quantities of soft drinks, but the boys in line with their much greater energy needs take larger amounts of cakes and biscuits.

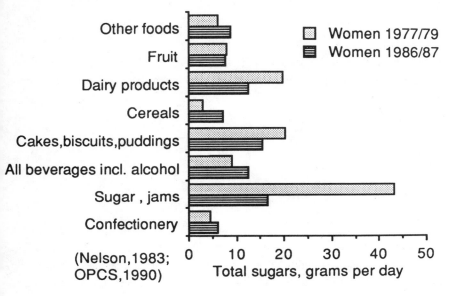

Figure 7. Total sugars intake by food groups of adult women in 1977/79 and 1986/87.

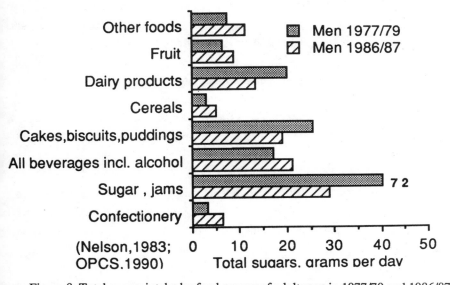

Figure 8. Total sugars intake by food groups of adult men in 1977/70 and 1986/87.

Figures 7 and 8 compare Nelson's 1977/79 survey [5] with the 1986/87 OPCS survey of

British adults [15]. Again, conclusions have to be made with caution as methodologies are different. With one exception the general pattern of food sources remains unchanged. There has been however a clear reduction in the amount of table sugar taken. The OPCS survey has therefore reflected the secular trend in purchases of packet sugar. Unlike the children, soft drinks are of lesser importance.

In summary the main sources of sugars in the diet are soft drinks, table sugar, confectionery and cakes, biscuits and puddings. Jams and breakfast cereals provide only small amounts.

Dietary counselling.

A. Is sugar bad for you?

In recent years several factors have come together to give the general public an exaggerated picture of sugar as a bad food.

First, the nutritionally sound advice given by dietitians to exclude sugar and sugar containing foods from reducing diets has generated a perception among the general public of sugar as having special fattening properties. This view is clearly unsound in that a calorie from sugar provides no more energy than a calorie from any food. The COMA committee concluded that "Dietary sugars may contribute to the general excess food energy consumption responsible for the development of obesity." but that "Omission of sugars from the diet...is not usually [of itself] sufficient as a weight-reducing regimen."

Second, the food activists have drawn attention to the presence of sugar in manufactured foods. This has had an adverse effect on health education in directing attention to a few foods such as jams and baked beans that make a very small contribution to the sugars intake. Concerns over the contribution of sugars from savoury foods seem quite unnecessary.

Finally there are the claims that sugar causes a wide variety of medical conditions from cardiovascular disease through diabetes to gall stones and bad behaviour. Three expert committees [1,16,17] have all concluded that this is not so, but the general public has not always received this message.

The case for recommending a reduction in sugar intake to the public in general (as opposed to those who need a reducing diet) rests solely on its proven cariogenic properties.

This raises the controversies over the importance of sugar in causing caries in the fluoride era, and the arguments about the cariogenic properties of starch, fermentable carbohydrates in general and starch/sugar mixtures as found in real foods. These controversies are not the topic of this paper, but they have a bearing on my view as a practical dieititian.

B. How can sugar be cut out of the diet?

The first and most obvious way is to cut out sugar in tea and coffee or to replace it with sweeteners. This is already happening and is probably partly responsible for the drop in packet sugar purchases.

Figure 9 shows that if all sugar taken as such was eliminated from the diets of the Cambridge men in 1977/79, the distribution would be very significantly shifted to the left and the long tail of high intakes would disappear. Since the OPCS survey of adults in 1986/87 [15] found 30 to 55 percent of those studied still took sugar in tea or coffee, there is scope for this simple action.

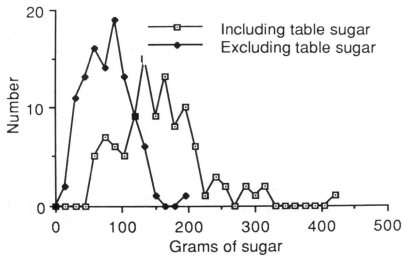

Figure 9. Distribution of total sugars intake in Cambridge men in 1977/79 including and excluding table sugar.

Second one can recommend drinking water instead of sugared drinks. Many mothers automatically give squash or fruit juice to their children. However, since soft drinks are often taken in a social situation where water would not be an appropriate alternative, diet versions can be substituted. This applies particularly to teenagers and to adults looking for an alternative to alcohol.

For confectionery there is a limited range of sugarless varieties on the market. The main option is that of limiting the quantity of sugar confectionery eaten.

For cakes and biscuits there is the option of limiting quantity; and many people do in fact eat very few. It is also possible to choose plainer varieties and some people already exercise this option. Unfortunately varieties low in sugar AND fat are limited to ones such as Ryvita, cream crackers, Rich Tea biscuits, currant buns, scones, and gingerbread. Bread and jam also has a lower sugar and lower fat content than many cakes and biscuits. All are fairly boring and none are sugarless.

The messages to the general public on how to reduce the amount of sugar in the diet are thus quite simple. But we have to ask, *if sugar is removed, what happens to the diet, and what foods are likely to replace the lost calories?* Not everyone needs to lose weight and many people are in appetite controlled energy balance.

Table 6 examines this question for the diets of the 18-year old males in Belfast. The first column gives the composition of the diet as measured. The second column gives the composition of the diet if all table sugar, soft drinks and confectionery were removed. This gives a good reduction in sugar intake. As a proportion of the diet of course all other components increase. Note particularly that the proportion of fat increases by 2 per cent.

TABLE 6.
Effect on nutrient balance of removing sugar containing foods from the diets of 18-year old Belfast boys and of replacing all the lost calories with bread and jam.

	Usual diet	Less sugar drinks sweets	Less cake biscuits puddings	Plus bread and jam
Energy,kcal	3680	3215	2495	3680
% energy from				
protein	11.5	12.6	14.6	12.4
fat	40.6	42.5	42.6	38.3
starch	21.5	24.1	23.5	30.2
added sugars	12.3	6.3	2.2	7.1
Energy lost, kcal		465	1185	
Dry bread equiv.		5.7 sl.	14.5 sl.	
Boiled potato eqiuv.		9 pots.	30 pots.	
Bread & jam equiv.		3.2 sl.	8.2 sl.	

This exercise also loses 465 calories from the diet. How are they to be replaced? If they are replaced by eating larger quantities of the diet that is left, then this is bad news in terms of recommended dietary guidelines for fat. Dietary guidelines would have us replace the lost sugar with complex carbohydrate. *The only foods which provide starch and no fat or sugar are bread and potatoes, rice and pasta.* The quantities of bread or potatoes required to replace the lost energy in the boys' diet are also shown. They are not small. It also has to be recognised that, even at a main meal, the British are not keen on dry bread. It is certainly not an attractive alternative to the snack foods favoured by today's youngsters!

Some typical snack foods that dentists would consider undesirable include Kit-Kat, Mars bars, chocolate biscuits, and muesli biscuits. Typical snacks that are not high sugar are crisps, Wotsits and similar products, peanuts, and Twiglets. Of these only Twiglets could conceivably be called low fat and even they contain 12 per cent.

It does seem particularly difficult to increase the complex carbohydrate content of the diet. When dietitians made a determined effort to eat according to dietary guidelines [10] they were unable in the short term to increase their intake of complex carbohydrate sufficiently to compensate for the calories lost by reducing fat intake. There was a shortfall of 300-400 calories. Two other studies had similar results [18,19]. All remarked particularly on the difficulty of finding low fat, low sugar snack foods. It may also be difficult even in the longer term.

A two year study of dietary intervention for breast cancer with advice to reduce fat and increase carbohydrates reported that subjects had lost weight at the follow-up after one year, and had not fully regained original weight at the end of the second year [20].

There are thus a number of practical problems associated with any attempt to limit consumption of high sugar cake, biscuit and snack foods. I also find sufficient confusion in the literature over the relative cariogenicity of real foods in real mouths in real life to have difficulty in saying with conviction that someone would be better off eating a Rich Tea biscuit than a Kit Kat.

At the present time a low sugar diet is still likely to be a higher fat diet. There are few indications that the population has achieved any reduction in the fat level of the diet. The proportion of the diet derived from protein, fat and carbohydrate as measured by the National Food Survey has remained unaltered for more than 10 years. I therefore do not consider that the primary message should be a reduction in the total *quantity* of sugars in the diet. Dental disease is undesirable, but heart disease is a killer.

68

For my dietary counselling therefore I come back to emphasis on limiting the *frequency* of sugars consumption. This has two very positive aspects. First, it is a simple message. Second, limiting frequency of consumption will automatically lower the very highest intakes that come from frequent cups of tea or soft drinks.

As a final thought, I suggest that we have all got our dietary advice wrong. I suggest that we should forget complicated messsages to cut fat and sugar and concentrate instead on promoting bread and potatoes. We should find an image for bread as the all essential staff of life and take up the French habit of eating it at all meals. If bread consumption increased and appetite took care of the calorie intake, then the levels of both fat and sugar in the diet would automatically be lowered.

TABLE 7.
Dietary advice to counter dental caries.

1.Limit the frequency of eating preferably to three times   per day or, at most, not more than six.

2. Avoid frequent snacking at less than hourly intervals.

3. Choose sugar free drinks for in-between meals.
Take tea or coffee without sugar or with non-sugar sweeteners. (NB Keep fat intake down by drinking it black or with skim or semi-skim milk)
Take diet versions of soft drinks.

4. Adopt the French habit of eating bread (without butter) with all meals.

REFERENCES

1. Committee on Medical Aspects of Food Policy. Dietary sugars in human disease. Reports on Health and Social Subjects 37. HMSO, London, 1989.

2. Ministry of Agriculture, Fisheries and Food. Household food consumption and expenditure, 1988: annual report of the National Food Survey Committee. HMSO, London, 1989.

3. Rugg-Gunn, A.J.,Hackett, A.F., Appleton, D.R. and Moynihan, P.J., The dietary intake of added and natural sugars in 405 English adolescents. Hum. Nut: Appl. Nutr., 1986, 40A, 115-124.

4. Hackett,A.F., Rugg-Gunn, A.J., Appleton, D.R., Eastoe, J.E. and Jenkins, G.N., A 2-year longitudinal nutritional survey of 405 Northumberland children initially aged 11.5 years. Br. J. Nutr. 1984, 51, 67-75.

5. Nelson, N., A dietary survey method for measuring family food purchases and individual nutrient intakes concurrently, and its use in dietary surveillance. PhD Thesis, University of London, 1983.

6. FAO/WHO/UNU, Energy and protein requirements. Wld Hlth Org. Techn. Rep. Ser. **724.** World Health Organisation, Geneva, 1985.

7. Schofield, W.S., Predicting basal metabolic rate, new standards and review of previous work. Hum. Nutr: Clin. Nutr. 1985, **39C,** Suppl. 1, 5-41.

8. Gibney, M.J., and Lee, P., Patterns of food and nutrient intake in the chronically unemployed consuming high and low levels of table sugar. Proc. Nutr. Soc. 1989, **48,** 132A.

9. Black, A.E., Ravenscroft, C. and Sims, A.J., The NACNE Report: are the dietary goals realistic? Comparisons with the dietary patterns of dietitians. Hum. Nutr: Appl. Nutr. 1984, **38A,** 165-179.

10. Cole-Hamilton, I., Gunner, K., Leverkus, C. and Starr, J.A., A study among dietitians and adult members of their households of the practicalities and implications of following proposed dietary guidelines for the UK. Hum. Nutr: Appl. Nutr. 1986, **40A,** 365-389.

11. Doyle, W., Sanderson, M. and Wynn, A.H.A., Nutrient intakes of high- and low-sugars consumers during pregnancy. Proc. Nutr. Soc. 1989, **48,** 46A.

12. Gibney, M., Moloney, M. and Shelley, E., The Kilkenny Health Project: food and nutrient intakes in randomly selected healthy adults. Br. J. Nutr. 1989, **61,** 129-137.

13. Nelson, M., Nutritional goals from COMA and NACNE: how can they be achieved? Hum. Nutr: Appl. Nutr. 1985, **39A,** 456-464.

14. Cade, J. and Booth, S., What can people eat to meet the dietary goals: and how much does it cost? J. Hum. Nutr. Diet. 1990, **3,** 199-207.

15. Gregory,J., Foster,K., Tyler,H. and Wiseman,M., The dietary and nutritional survey of British adults. HMSO, London, 1990.

16. Glinsmann, W.H., Irausquin, H. and Park, Y.K., Evaluation of health aspects of sugars contained in carbohydrate sweeteners: report of Sugars Taskforce. J. Nutr. 1986, **116,** S1-S216.

17. British Nutrition Foundation., Sugars and syrups: the report of the British Nutrition Foundation's Task Force. BNF, London, 1987.

18. Bradley, A. and Theobald, A., The effects of dietary modification as defined by NACNE on the eating habits of 28 people. J. Hum. Nutr. Diet. 1988, **1,** 105-114.

19. Warwick, P.M. and Williams, L.T., Dietary intake of individuals interested in eating a healthy diet: a validated study of intake before and after dietary advice. Hum. Nutr: Appl. Nutr. 1987, **41A,** 409-425.

20. Nordevang, E., Ikkala, E., Callmer, E., Hallstrom, L. and Holm, L.-E., Dietary intervention in breast cancer patients: effects on dietary habits and nutrient intake. Europ. J. Clin. Nutr. 1990, **44,** 681-687.

SUGARS, SWEETENERS and DENTAL CARIES PREVENTION

Monique TRILLER
Faculté de Chirurgie Dentaire (Paris V)
1, rue Maurice Arnoux
92120 - Montrouge
France

ABSTRACT

Caries is a microbial disease which induces the destruction of the calcified tissues of the teeth. Loss of substance are linked to acid production which is the result of the degradation of dietary carbohydrates by the microorganisms of the oral cavity. In the mouth, each sugar intake is rapidly followed by a pH fall which can be compensated by the buffer capacity of saliva. Phases of de- and remineralization occur permanently in the oral cavity. However, if bacteria or carbohydrates are in excess (poor oral hygiene and/or diet desequilibrium) or if salivary factors are deficient (general pathologies or therapies), a pathologic context will occur in an irreversible way. Caries prevention involves therefore the control of the diet (frequency, amount, consistency and time of carbohydrates ingestion). It is almost impossible to forbid strictly sugar intake. For this reason, sugar substitues or synthetic sweeteners can be very useful. In vitro and in vivo studies have shown that these substances are little metabolised by oral microorganisms and that their use is not followed by acid production.

INTRODUCTION

Caries is a microbial disease which destroys progressively the calcified tissues of the teeth by acid demineralization (fig. 1 & 2). Acid production, particularly lactic acid, is the result of the degradation of dietary carbohydrates by the microorganisms present in the oral cavity.

Dental caries is generally considered only as a painful disease which, in the absence of therapy, will result in loss of tooth substance, and with further functional and/or esthetic prejudice.

Fig. 1 : Carious enamel :
demineralization of the
prisms by acid produced by
the oral microorganisms

Fig. 2 : Carious dentine :
the demineralization of the
tissue allows bacterial
penetration into the dentine

According to W.H.O., oral pathologies (caries and perio-
dontal diseases) are the 3rd cause of morbidity in the world.
On the other hand, for patients presenting general pathologies such as heart diseases, rheumatism , irradiation therapies, nephropathies, etc., streptococcal septicity linked to
active caries lesions must be considered as a major risk.

It is essential then, not only to develop dental care,
but also to promote programs of prevention in order to limit
the extension of caries into the population.

The programs on caries prevention aim to

- reinforce enamel resistance to acid attack
  (fluoride therapies)

- promote oral hygiene

- educate patients for diet equilibrium

72

The present data intend to report upon :
1) the relationship between sugar consumption and caries
   pathogenesis
2) the alternative possibility of non cariogenic
   sweeteners

PATHOGENESIS OF DENTAL CARIES

The process of demineralization of the hard tissus of the
teeth is the consequence of repeated periods of low pH inside
the oral cavity.

The oral cavity is an heterogenous medium where are present together constitutive structural elements and both
variable endogenous and exogenous factors. The structural
elements concerned here are the teeth. The variable endogenous factors are the salivary secretions and the variable
exogenous factors are the elements entering the oral cavity
such as atmospheric elements and food products (1) (fig. 3)

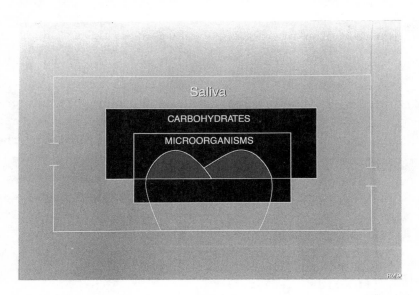

Figure 3 : schematic representation of the factors which
interact in the pathogenesis of caries.

Furthermore, the oral cavity is a septic reservoir of microorganisms, particularly Streptococci and Actinomyces (2).

As soon as the teeth erupt, salivary glycoproteins are
adsorbed on enamel surface and constitute the acquired
pellicle. It is through this pellicle that the bacteria
are going to adhere to enamel surfaces (fig. 4). In the
absence of oral hygiene, bacterial growth will ensure the
formation of the dental plaque.

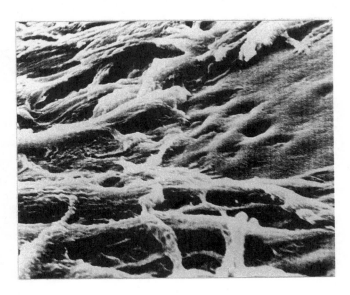

Figure 4 : Early bacterial colonization on the surface of
newly erupted enamel

The microorganisms will accumulate particularly in the
areas where tooth brushing is difficult, such as pits and
fissures, linked to tooth morphology, interdental spaces,
iatrogenic restorations etc.

When food is ingested, the bacteria will metabolise
the carbohydrates which are necessary for their energy
(fig. 5). The extracellular degradation products are :
    1) lactic acid
    2) insoluble polysaccharides (dextrans and levans).

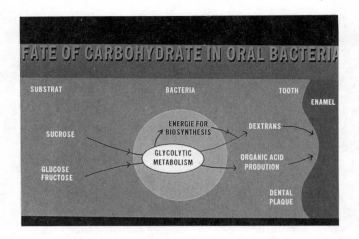

Figure 5 :   Schematic representation of the metabolism of
carbohydrate by bacteria

Lactic acid and subsequent fall of pH at the enamel-
plaque interface will break down the hydroxyapatite crystals
of enamel. Extracellular polysaccharides will contribute to
bacterial aggregation on tooth surfaces and growth of the
plaque.

However, each sugar intake is not systematically followed
by a carious lesion !

The first reaction when the pH falls around 5.5 is :

$$Ca_{10}(PO_4)6(OH)_2 + 2H^+ \longrightarrow 3Ca_3(PO_4)_2 + Ca^{++} + 2H_2O$$

This represents the first stage of demineralization. At this
stage only 10% of the calcium of the tooth has become soluble.
If the reaction stops, or if the pH rises, the calcium
phosphate can reprecipitate on enamel surface; from Ca and
PO_4 ions solubilized from the previous reaction and from
mineral ions present in the saliva, and be reconverted into
apatite.

But if the pH continues to fall below 5.5, tricalcium
phosphate will break down to dicalcium phosphate, then with
a greater concentration of hydrogen ions, the apatite will

completely dissolve :

$$Ca_{10}(PO_4)6(OH)_2 + 14H \longrightarrow 10Ca + 6H_2PO_4 + 2H_2O$$

Salivary factors are able to regulate these reactions :

1) The salivary secretions contribute to eliminate food and bacterial debris from the tooth surfaces.

2) Enzymes and immunoglobulins present in the saliva inhibit bacterial metabolism.

3) Buffer capacity of the saliva modulates pH variations.

4) Mineral ions present in saliva (Ca and PO_4) are able to reprecipitate on enamel.

When the situation is equilibrated, enamel undergoes phases of de- and remineralization which are compatible with good dental health.

The situation will become pathological and irreversible when this equilibrium is broken down, and when the phases of demineralization predominate either :

- because pathogenic factors (poor oral hygiene and sugar consumption) are in excess

- because regulation factors are poor (salivary parameters).

SUGAR INTAKE AND CARIES

Relationship between sugar intake and caries is well known from epidemiological surveys or animal experimentations (3-4-5) (fig. 6).

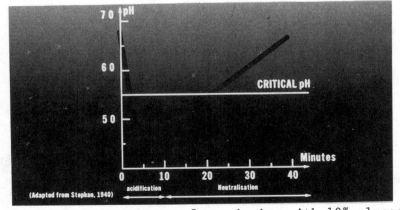

Figure 6 : pH of the plaque after rinsing with 10% glucose solution

For example, during the 2nd World War, when sugar consumption was low, a fall in caries prevalence has been observed in spite of severe food restrictions (6-7).

The changes of traditional dietary habits into a carbohydrate rich "occidental" type of food has induced a severe increase of caries prevalence among Esquimos or Polynesian populations where caries were almost unknown as long as these populations had remained isolated (8).

On the other hand, the children who possess an hereditary fructose intolerance and who are submitted to a strict diet, do not develop caries even if their oral hygiene is poor (9).

In industrialized countries, the changes which have occured in life habits have modified simultaneously dietary behaviour. Higher and higher consumption of snacks and soft drinks has resulted in an increase in caries prevalence.

Animal experimentations confirm the close relationship between high sugar intake and caries. From the feeding machine introduced by König (10), it is possible to correlate a particular type of food, amount and frequency of ingestion and the score of caries.

The relationship between dietary carbohydrates and caries production is determined by a combination of several factors which are :
- the chemical nature of the sugar and its potential to be metabolized by oral bacteria and consequently the amount of acid production (11)
  - the quantity of sugar intake
  - the concentration of sugar in various types of food
  - the frequency of ingestion (12)
  - the consistency and adherence to the tooth surfaces (13)
  - the rate of diffusion into the plaque (14)
  - the moment of ingestion

The comparative cariogenicity of the different carbohydrates versus their physicochemical properties is related to their molecular weight : macromolecules with a high molecular weight such as starch are less cariogenic than low molecular weight molecules such as sucrose, glucose, lactose or maltose which are rapidly metabolized.

Furthermore, starch must be hydrolysed into smaller units before it can enter and diffuse into the plaque.

The cariogenicity of sugars is also related to the bacterial metabolism and the ability of the bacteria to ferment dietary carbohydrates.

The two major specific microorganisms considered responsible for carious process are Streptococcus Mutans (primary initiator) and Lactobacillus Acidophilus (secondary extender) (15). They both readily ferment sugar to acid. S.Mutans has also the ability to synthetize and store extracellular complex carbohydrates (dextrans and levans) for future fermentation. These polysaccharides provide also a sticky coating which contributes to the growth of the plaque and its adhesion to the tooth surfaces.

The kinetics of the carious process is related to the rate of the degradation and metabolism of carbohydrates by the microorganisms in the oral cavity : highly concentrated and readily fermentable mono- and disaccharides which diffuse quickly into the plaque are more cariogenic than large, insoluble, non-diffusable polysaccharide molecules.

The longer a carbohydrate cariogenic food remains in contact with the surface of enamel, the greater will be the probability for longer periods of acid production at the plaque-enamel interface. Marked differences in sugar clearance are observed whether the food is chewed (cake), sucked (toffee) or drunk (16).

The cariogenicity of a food product is directly related:

1) to the amount of time during which this product will remain adherent to the tooth and will therefore allow long periods of bacterial metabolism which will induce acid production and enamel demineralization ;

2) to the time of ingestion : in between meals or before sleeping sugar intake, when salivary secretion is low, creates a more potential cariogenic situation than when sugar is ingested during the meals.

NON-CARIOGENIC SWEETENERS

There is evidence which indicates that most people enjoy
sweet food. One can speculate whether this preference for
sweets is innate or learned. Babies seem happy when drinking
sugar-flavoured water. Later in life taste preference for
sweets can be increased by family food habits (17).

Dietary recommendations concering caries prevention
must be practical and realistic. It is almost impossible to
forbid strictly sugar intake (18-19). In order to help and
encourage the patients trying to reduce their amount of
sugar consumption, a good alternative is the use of sugar
substitutes in candies, chewing gums or soft drinks. These
substitutes confer sweetness to the food in which they are
incorporated, but do not produce acid when they are fermented
by the bacterial plaque. The characteristics and properties
of non-cariogenic sweeteners have been detailed in textbooks
(3-4).

Sugar substitutes can be divided in non-nutritive and
nutritive sweeteners.

Non-nutritive sweeteners are synthetic substances.
Their sweetening property is high compared to sucrose. They
provide no calories and are safe for teeth. They are mainly :
- Cyclamate
- Saccharin
- Aspartame

Nutritive sweeteners are mostly sugar alcohols named
also polyols. They are manufactured from natural products.
They are mainly :
- Sorbitol, which can be produced commercially from
sucrose or starch
- Mannitol, obtained by the hydrogenation of mannose
- Xylitol, which derives from various types of cellulose
products and which can also be produced from the wood of
birch trees
- Lycasin, which derives from hydrogenation of starch.

These polyols are regarded as less cariogenic than
sucrose. Their cariogenicity can be evaluated from <u>in vitro</u>

and _in vivo_ experimentation based on the measurement of bacterial growth and metabolism (ability to produce lactic acid), fall in the pH of the plaque (acid production from salivary fermentation).

- _In vitro_ studies indicate that the growth of Streptococcus mutans on culture medium depends on the composition of the substrate : when the medium is supplemented with Sorbitol or Mannitol, the bacterial growth is much lower than when the medium is supplemented with glucose. It is completely inhibited in presence of Xylitol or Lycasin (20).

- pH fall and lactic acid production measured in the culture medium are less important in presence of Sorbitol or Mannitol compared with glucose-supplemented medium. There is no production of lactic acid in presence of Xylitol or Lycasin (20).

Cariogenicity of sweet foods containing polyols versus foods containing glucose can be evaluated _in vivo_ by intra-oral pH telemetry : Plaque pH from interdental areas is measured by the use of a telemetric partial prosthesis. During the test period, which allows plaque to grow over the tip of the electrodes, the intradental plaque is exposed to fermentable carbohydrates. The pH changes resulting from the acid formed are measured. From this technique, the following parameters can be measured :
- permeability of plaque to carbohydrates
- buffer activity of plaque environment
- effect of dietary carbohydrate on pH

The results indicate that polyols do not induce pH fall below 5.5 and therefore can be considered "safe" for the teeth (21) (fig. 7).

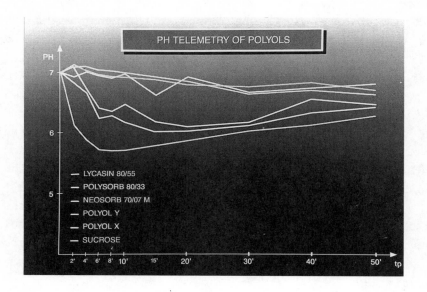

Figure 7 : Results of pH telemetry of polyols versus sucrose.

Fermentation and acid production of polyols versus glucose can be tested in vitro : pH variations are measured in a culture medium added with human saliva and the product to be tested. During the test period (21 hours), the supplemented medium is incubated at 33°C. Measurements are made at regular intervals. The results give a curve of the pH values. Fall of pH below 5.5 indicates that the product must be considered as cariogenic (22) (fig. 8-9-10-11).

81

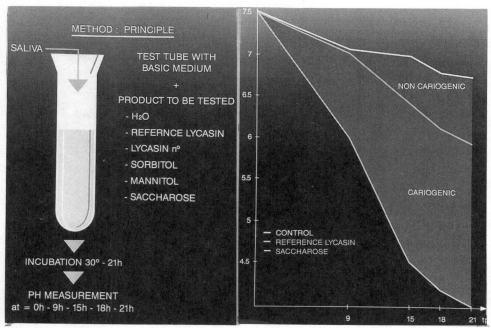

Fig.8: _In vitro_ measurement of
acidogenic power.

Fig. 9 : Results

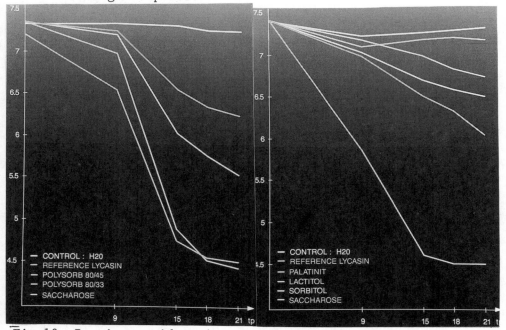

Fig.10: _In vitro_ acidogenic
properties of polyols

Fig.11: _In vitro_ acidogenic
properties of polyols

It is unrealistic to ask a patient to give up sugar
completely. Dietary advice is rarely followed even when
repeated instructions are given on the relationship between
amount and frequency of sugar intake and caries.

From both _in vivo_ and _in vitro_ tests it appears that
polyols can be considered as "safe for the teeth" as long as
pH fall, in presence of polyols, does not reach the critical
point of 5.5 under which demineralization of enamel occurs.
They can be usefully incorporated into food, beverages or
prescriptions to which they will give a sweet taste. Therefore polyol — containing products constitute a good alternative to glucose-containing products for those individuals who
have a strong preference for sweet tasting food.

Caries prevention involves together oral hygiene,
fluoride therapies and diet equilibrium. Non-cariogenic
sweeteners are part of the panel which can contribute to
better dental health among the population.

REFERENCES

1. Triller, M., La carie dentaire. _La Recherche_, 1981,
   800-809

2. Geddes, D.A.M., The production of lactic acid and volatile
   acids by human dental plaque and the effect of plaque
   buffering and acid strength on pH. _Arch. Oral Biol._, 1972,
   17, 537-545.

3. Nizel : Nutrition in preventive dentistry.
   W.B. Saunders Cie., 1981.

4. Report on Health and Social Subjects : 37 : Dietary Sugars
   and Human Disease. HMSO Pub.Ctr., London, 1989.

5. Marthaler T.M. : Epidemiological and clinical dental
   findings in relation to intake of carbohydrates.
   Caries Res., 1967, 1, 222.

6. Toverud G. : Decrease in caries frequency in Norvegian
   children during World War II. _J.A.D.A._, 1949, 39, 127

7. Sogannaes R.F. : Analyses of wartime reduction of dental
   caries in European children. _Amer. J. Dis. Child._, 1948,
   75, 792.

8. Rosebury T. and Waugh L.M. : Dental caries among Eskimos
   of the Kuskokovim area of Alaska. Am. J.Dis.Child.,
   1939, 58, 191

9. Marthaler T.M. and Froesch E.R. : Hereditary fructose
   intoleance. Dental status of eight patients. Brit. Dent.
   J. 1967, 123, 197.

10. König K.G. : Caries activity induced by frequency-
    controlled feedings of diet containing sucrose or bread
    to Osborne-Mendel rats. Arch. Oral Biol., 1969,14,991.

11. Edgar W.M. et al. : Acid production in plaque after
    eating snacks ; modifying factors in food. J. Amer.Dent.
    Ass., 1975, 90, 418.

12. Lundquist C. : Oral sugar clearance. Odont. Revy
    (suppl. 1) 1952, 1.

13. Caldwell R.C. : Physical properties of food and their
    caries-producing potential. J. Dent. Res., 1970,49,1293.

14. Edgar W.M. : Effect of sequence in food intake on plaque
    pH. Conf. on food,nutrition and dental health : Role of
    Sugar and the Foods in Dental Caries. Res. Inst. Amer.
    Dent. Hlth Foundation, 1978, 90-96.

15. Brown A.T. : The role of dietary carbohydrates in plaque
    formation and oral disease. Nutr. Rev., 1975, 33,353-361

16. Volker J.F. : Relation of oral biochemistry of sugars
    to the development of caries. J. Amer. Dent. Ass.
    1955, 51, 285.

17. Beidler L.M. : The biological and cultural role of
    sweeteners. in : "Sweeteners and Dental Caries" eds.
    Shaw J.H., Roussos G.C., Information Retrivieval Inc.,
    Washington D.C., 1978.

18. Murray J.J. : The prevention of dental diseases.
    Oxford Univ. Press, 1983.

19. Nikiforuk G. : Understanding dental caries. S.Karger,
    Basel, 1985.

20. Soyer G. and Frank R.M. : Influence du milieu de culture
    sur la croissance de Streptococcus Mutans ATCC 25175
    en présence de différents glucides et de leurs dérivés.
    J. Biol. Buccale, 1979, 9 (3), 295-301.

21. T.N. Imfeld : Identification of low caries risk dietary
    components. Monographs in Oral Sci., vol. 11, ed. Karger,
    1983.

84

22. Benaich O. and Maarek H. : Le lycasin 80/55, sucre de substitution dans la prévention de la carie dentaire. Thèse pour le Doctorat en Chirurgie Dentaire, Paris V, 1990.

CONFECTIONERY APPLICATIONS AND MARKETING IN SWITZERLAND

JEAN-CLAUDE SALAMIN
Group Product Manager/Chocolate Division
Société des Produits Nestlé SA
P.O. Box 352, 1800 Vevey, CH

ABSTRACT

Sugarless sweets that are kind to the teeth first appeared in Switzerland in 1969. Their development was at first slow to take off. To combat this lack of confidence on the part of the consumer, the Swiss Sympadent association, a collaboration between university dentistry departments, the raw materials industry and the finished-products industry, was founded in 1982. The "smiling tooth" logo was soon invented and duly protected, highlighting the non-cariogenic and "kind to teeth" qualities of those products. Under the aegis of the Sympadent association, the industry financed educational advertising campaigns aimed at encouraging the public to practice preventive measures in the domain of oral health. For we must admit, that the health of the teeth is not just a question of consuming sugarless products. Essentially it is a result of the strict implementation of a range of preventive measures.

THE ARRIVAL OF SUGARLESS SWEETS

Sugarless sweets that are kind to the teeth first appeared in Switzerland in 1969. Their arrival was the fruit of collaboration between industrialist and confectionery manufacturer, Mr. Alfred Disch; a professor of dentistry at the University of Zürich, who has devoted his life to prevention in the field of oral hygiene, Professor Mühlemann; and, last but not least, a supplier of raw materials, Roquette Frères.

Technical development

Motivated by personal commitment and spurred on by the realism that made him successful, the head of the Disch corporation developed "Happy" sweets, which we still sell today in improved versions. With standard production equipment at his disposal, he needed a raw material that could be processed in the same way as sugar and glucose syrup. This material was Lycasin. Delivered in syrup form, it needed only to be concentrated, cooked, flavoured and shaped using existing equipment.

Although processing of the new raw material was easy, its flavouring presented some problems: indeed, in place of flavour-bearing fruit extracts it was necessary to substitute pure flavours, using alcohol or essential oils as a medium. However, the quality of those available at the time left much to be desired. Today this handicap has been overcome.

The sweets produced then, of quite acceptable quality, passed the "in vivo" telemetry test and thus obtained the "zahnschonend" label. This label is awarded by the Federal Public Health Service if the pH level of dental plaque does not fall below 5.7 within 30 minutes of the sweet being eaten.

Initial marketing approach

In a stagnant market, the development of sugarless sweets was at first slow to take off. Being the only operator in the market, the Disch company had difficulty in making its voice heard. The appearance of rival products stimulated the market. Nevertheless, ten years after the launch of the first sugarless sweets, and despite the incessant attacks made on products containing sugar, their share of the confectionery market was only a modest 5%.

There are several reasons for this lack of interest in sugarless sweets:
. The taste quality of the products was no match for that of products containing sucrose.
. The price was high, owing to the high cost of basic materials and the aluminium packaging needed to counteract the hygroscopicity of the product.
. The lack of information among the public about the health benefits of products that were kind to the teeth.
. Suspicion of an ingredient felt by the consumer to be artificial.
. The fact that the sugarless sweet in a sense ran contrary to the whole idea of what a sweet was.

CREATION OF THE SYMPADENT ASSOCIATION

Aims, activities

The Sympadent confectionery association, a collaboration between university dentistry departments, the raw materials industry and the finished-products, chewing gum and confectionery industry, was founded in 1982 to combat this lack of confidence on the part of the consumer. The association began by inventing and duly protecting the "smiling tooth" logo, highlighting the non-cariogenic and "kind to teeth" qualities of those products which were authorized to be marked in this way.

A public relations operation set out to spread awareness of the acronym, in particular through articles in the daily press and periodicals. At the same time, an advertising campaign in the press attempted to make the public better acquainted with the sugar substitutes used in sugarless sweets and chewing-gums, and hence to increase their acceptance. Leaflets distributed through paediatricians and dentists carried the same message, supplemented with advice on oral hygiene.

The advertising campaign, directed initially at mothers, switched to children, leaving the press in favour of television. Running alongside the advertising campaigns, exhibitions successfully toured the country under the title "Tooth decay can be avoided", and brought the message into schools and shopping centres. They were intended mainly for schoolchildren and teachers, and stressed that the health of the teeth and gums could be protected in three ways:

. good oral hygiene

. use of fluoridated toothpaste

. consumption of products with a low sugar content, in particular sugarless sweets

Image, awareness, and attitudes study

In 1986 and 1989 the Swiss Sympadent association carried out a study with the IHA-GFM Institute, the main aims of which were to ascertain public awareness of understanding of the acronym "Sympadent", acceptance of the taste of sugarless products, their image, and attitudes towards them. These are the main results:

Awareness:
A high rate of awareness, with 68% of the population recognising the symbol, rising to 78% of women and 93% of young people between the ages of 15 and 19.

Origin of awareness:
When asked where they had seen the Sympadent symbol, 81% of those who recognised it had seen it on products.

Products recognised bearing the symbol:
73% saw it on packets of chewing-gum
64% saw it on packets of sweets
12% saw it on chocolates

Appreciation of the taste of sugarless products:
Positive appreciation, with 78% considering the taste of sugarless sweets to be very good and good; this rose to 86% in the 15-19 age group.

Image of Sympadent products
Based on a 5 point semantic differential paired scale, the attribute "less harmful for teeth", with a score of 1.7, is appreciated most widely, followed by "do not cause decay" and "do not have many calories" with 1.9.

With an average of 3.3, Toothfriendly products are considered to be expensive.

There is, on the other hand, indifference concerning the following attributes:
have a natural flavour - have an artificial flavour
have a typical flavour - have an unnatural flavour
are not sweet enough   - are too sweet

Health image of sugarless sweets

It was felt necessary to find out whether the use of sugar substitutes to replace sugar was regarded as without risk to the health, or whether they were believed to represent a health hazard.

47% of those asked (54% of 15-19 year-olds) think there is no health risk.

27% (24% of 15-19 year-olds) do feel there is a health risk.

Intention to buy sugarless products

Interest in buying sugarless sweets shows a downward trend, with only 16% of people compared with 23% in 1986 buying sugarless sweets only; 48% compared with 51% in 1986 only buy from time to time. This decline is in evidence across all age groups.

To summarize, these two studies show that:

. the Sympadent symbol has gained a high level of public awareness, particularly among women and young people, who are the main purchasers and consumers of sweets.

. the quality of Sympadent products is considered to be good.

. the Sympadent symbol conveys the image of products that protect the teeth and do not cause decay, and has the added attribute of low-calorie products.

. the inclination to buy sugarless products seems to be falling off and becoming less fashionable.

MARKETING APPLICATION

Trends

Thanks to better information and the dynamism and innovative approach of companies, sales of sugarless sweets have tripled in volume over the last decade. Today they represent just over 14% of the confectionery market, not including chewing-gum. This corresponds to a per capita consumption of 380 g per year. Nearly a hundred brands/varieties are contesting the market. Switzerland is thus well to the fore in the consumption of sugarless confectionery products.

This spectacular development is due to the following main factors:

. placing on the market of products in ever greater numbers, covering different market sectors.

. the constant improvement in the taste quality of sugarless sweets.

. the recent appearance of a promising gap in the market for sugarless

. sweets with reduced calories.

. varieties suitable for diabetics.

. the strong progress of media investment in favour of sugarless sweets, which today account for 28% of all confectionery advertising.

. availability of sugarless sweets in all distribution networks; from kiosks to large stores, from bakery to grocery shops.

. the trend in favour of "light" (calorie reduced) products, helping to prevent weight problems.

It is very interesting to note that in the chewing-gum sector, the share of sugarless products is 50%. Sugarless chewing-gum is now incontestably at the forefront of products that are kind to the teeth. On the other hand, the share of sugarless products in the chocolate market is negligible. This is due to the fact that sugarless chocolate has never attained a level of quality acceptable to the consumer. After all, chocolate is essentially a product which affords the consumer pleasure. Deprived of their pleasure, consumers have turned away from sugarless chocolate.

In the chocolate and confectionery market overall (including chewing-gum) the share of sugarless products is in the region of 5%.

Opportunities

Sugarless sweets in pocket-size packets today constitute a promising new gap in the Swiss market. These sweets, in the form of small pearls, drops, soft or hard pastilles, come in a wide range of flavours: mint, eucalyptus, herbs, fruits, etc. They are packaged in 20 to 45 g boxes and sold at a high price, mainly to adults. With these products, all of the

consumer's motivations and expectations are satisfied:
. convenient, practical packaging
. unobtrusive product
. kind to teeth
. light, good for the figure
. refreshing to eat
. substitute for cigarettes
. eases the conscience
. frees from feelings of guilt

The innovations in this sector are by no means yet exhausted.

OUTLOOKS

Today, the feeling in the industry is that the sugarless confectionery market has come of age. A slowing down in growth is foreseeable mainly for the following reasons:

. people who care about healthy teeth also care about a healthy body. The information which it has recently become obligatory to include on packaging, according to which sugarless sweets may have a laxative effect when consumed in excess in a short period of time, will tend to dissuade people from eating these products. We have already received some complaints on this point. A study of this question carried out in July 1990 by the MIS Institute in Lausanne, reveals that 57% of consumers would not change their buying habits, 22% would cut down their consumption, and 21% would stop eating sugarless sweets.

. the downward trend in the consumption of traditional confectionery products.

. the restoring to favour of sugar, which today is no longer considered to be a health hazard.

92

CONCLUSIONS

The marketing success of sugarless sweets in Switzerland is without doubt the result of close collaboration between confectionery manufacturers and raw materials suppliers on the one hand, and university dentistry institutes on the other.

Confectionery manufacturers have understood, certainly not without some initial hesitation, that what was at stake was not an open war against products containing sugar, but rather the possibilty of giving consumers an alternative by offering a choice between products with sugar and those without. Sugar confectionery and oral disease were therefore regarded as a major challenge, to which they could contribute in finding a solution by seeking ways of converting these problems into opportunities.

It is with this in mind that they have, on the one hand, developed a very diverse range of sugarless confectionery that is kind to the teeth, and on the other hand, under the aegis of the Sympadent association, financed educational advertising campaigns aimed at encouraging the public to practice preventive measures in the domain of oral health.

Today, Swiss schoolchildren experience less than a third of the tooth decay suffered by their elders thirty years ago, despite an increase in the consumption of chocolates and sugar. We must admit, therefore, that oral health is not just a question of consuming sugarless products. Essentially it is a result of the strict implementation of a range of preventive measures outlined above.

Pleasure and health go well together if reason prevails.

SUGARFREE APPLICATIONS AND MARKETING IN THE U.K.

PHILIP HAMILTON
Managing Director
The Wrigley Company Ltd.
Estover, Plymouth, Devon PL6 7PR

INTRODUCTION

For the next twenty minutes I propose to speak to you about the sugarfree applications and marketing in the U.K. confectionery market.

My talk will be broken down into three separate sections. First of all the size, growth and composition of the confectionery market. Secondly the different types of sugar free sweeteners available to the confectionery industry, and thirdly an example of an outstandingly successful sugarfree confectionery product.

THE U.K. CONFECTIONERY MARKET

The U.K. confectionery market is certainly one of the most sophisticated and developed confectionery markets in Western Europe as can be seen from the number of acquisitive predators which have shown such interest in our industry in the last few years. The total amount of confectionery consumed is in the region of 800,000 tonnes, and over the years if one looks back to 1954, has grown by 19% but has also significantly changed in composition. Whereas forty years ago the market was principally one of sugar confectionery, this has considerably declined and in the meantime the chocolate sector has developed to a dominant share. The total growth should really be looked at from a per-capita consumption basis since during this period the increase in population has been an important factor. Obviously there is a major reduction in the sugar confectionery from 7 kilos per annum in 1954 to 5.3 kilos per annum in 1989 and conversely there is an increase in chocolate confectionery from 5.7 kilos per annum to 8.4 kilos per annum in 1989. Combining these two sectors gives us an increase in the per-capita consumption of only 8% which is surprisingly low in the context of the amount of publicity and attention which this market attracts.

On a daily basis the average consumer consumes on average about 37 grams of confectionery per day, which is equivalent to, lets say, two snack bars a day. Quite obviously some consumers consume a great deal more and some consume none at all.

Within each sector, one can see that within sugar confectionery, boiled sweets have significantly declined from 38% to 21% whereas products such as mints, popcorn, nougat and liquorice, etc. have increased from 22% to 37%, all this within a declining sector share of the total confectionery market. In the chocolate sector, the most important changes have been in solid chocolate bars which have declined from 29% to 13% and the bite size sector such as assortments, boxes, etc. which has significantly reduced from 42% to 24%. On the other hand filled snack bars have increased significantly from 27% to 38% and the cereal bar sector, which didn't exist in 1954, now accounts for 18% of all sales. Both these sectors, therefore, are experiencing significant change in their composition with important shifts in consumer buying patterns towards new types of more innovative and attractive products. The other important changes which have taken place have been the increase in the frequency of snacking between meals, in some cases six to seven times per day, and the switch to younger consumers whose eating habits are less centred around the old ways of formal eating times.

Total purchases by consumers are valued in the region of £3 billion, and of this, only very few products, such as mints and chewing gum, are in a sugarfree form with a value of something in the region of £100m, or 3% of the total market. In the U.S.A., 10% of the market is now in sugarfree form.

In summary the U.K. confectionery market is certainly still growing. The chocolate sector is the only sector which is growing whilst sugar confectionery is on the decline and the per-capita consumption over a period of forty years has only increased by 8%. However, the frequency of snacking has increased and the consumer is younger than previously, whilst sugarfree products have yet to make an impact.

SUGARFREE SWEETENERS AND THEIR APPLICATION

The next section I would like to talk about is the various types of
sugarfree sweeteners which are available to the manufacturing industry.

Sugarless sweeteners can be divided into two major categories: sugar
alcohols or alditols which have low sweetness intensity, and high
intensity sweeteners.

Alditols are materials which are used in virtually all sugarless
confections but never in soft drinks. They provide bulk and mouth feel
similar to sucrose.

High Intensity Sweeteners are a chemically diverse group of
substances which range in sweetness from 20 to 5000 times sweeter than
sucrose. Because of this potency, they cannot replace the bulk and mouth
feel of sucrose and therefore are often combined with alditols in
applications where these properties are important. They are noncariogenic
and essentially noncaloric.

A major factor in the appeal of a confection is sweetness and the
quality of that sweetness. The consumer desires the same sweet taste
experienced in the sugar-sweetened counterpart without objectionable
aftertaste. Of the polyol alternative sweeteners, xylitol is the
sweetest. With the sweetness equivalent of 1.0, xylitol is isosweet to
sucrose followed in descending order by those of maltitol, sorbitol,
maltitol syrup, mannitol, isomalt and polydextrose which has negligible
sweetness. Sweetness synergism between the polyols can provide a
formulation benefit. For example, a 60:40 sweetener ratio of xylitol and
sorbitol in chewing gum, or an 80:20 sweetener ratio of maltitol and
xylitol in chocolate will produce sugarfree products which are essentially
isosweet to their sugar-sweetened counterparts.

The solubility of a bulk sweetener alternative can greatly influence
the perceived mouthfeel and texture of the final product. Solubility can
also affect the perception of sweetness onset. It is, therefore,
desirable that the alternative sweetener have a solubility profile similar
to sugar. Of the crystalline alternative sweeteners, xylitol, maltitol,
sorbitol and polydextrose exhibit solubilities equal to or greater than
sucrose.

Cost continues to be a major influence when selecting alternative
bulk sweeteners for use in sugarfree confections. On a dry solids basis,

maltitol syrup, for example, is about 5 times more expensive than the corn syrup it replaces. The commonly used sucrose replacer sorbitol is about 2 to 3 times more expensive than sugar. Mannitol, xylitol and, potentially, isomalt and maltitol are even more expensive.

While many consumers are turned away from sugarfree products because of the cost premium, it is possible that more are turned away because of unacceptable product sweeteness and texture.

In summary the number of sugarfree ingredients are quite diverse. All of them pose major manufacturing and organoleptic challenges if one wishes to produce high quality confectionery which is acceptable to the consuming public.

A SUGARFREE CONFECTIONERY PRODUCT

The third and final part of my talk concerns The Wrigley Company and its sugarfree business. The Wrigley Company is located in Devon, bordered on the one hand by the sea and on the other by Dartmoor National Park. The Wrigley Company has been selling chewing gum in the U.K since 1915 and sells exclusively chewing gum; having no other interest in any other types of products. The size of the company is relatively modest with a turnover in the region of £50m and about 500 employees.

The size of the chewing gum market in the U.K. at consumer buying prices is in the region of £90m, which is 3% or 4% of the total confectionery market and therefore makes us very modest players in a very big league. However, The Wrigley Company enjoys a market share in the region of 90%, in other words, 9 out of every 10 packets of chewing gum sold are Wrigley brands. The reason for this healthy market share is a dedication and focus on just one type of product and the recognition that point of sale display, merchandising and advertising are very important. Every day we make about 15 million sticks of chewing gum which is equivalent to Plymouth to Glasgow every day. We say sometimes that we make gum at 120 miles an hour. These 15 million sticks daily are bought by 20 million consumers and they can find these products in 95% of all grocery and newsagent outlets in the U.K. They will also find in 98% of those outlets that a Wrigley display stand is prominently displayed near the check-out since chewing gum today is a high impulse purchase product.

In the last 4 years, Wrigley sales, and therefore the total market, have been increasing significantly, and today stand very nearly 50% above

1986. There are several reasons for this. One is new advertising and at a much higher level. Secondly, much improved merchandising at a point of sale both of which have had a dramatic impact on sales, and thirdly, the availability of sugarfree products. In fact Orbit chewing gum, which is a sugarfree product, was introduced in 1976, and was really relatively insignificant for many years until it was reformulated in 1986 with the use of aspartame, encapsulation techniques for flavourings and new packaging. This was in effect a total reformulation and resulted in an outstanding product. As can be seen from this chart, in 1985 only 8% of our business was in sugarfree products, whereas by next year we fully anticipate that at least 32% of our business will be in sugarfree products. During this time the regular brands have continued to increase owing to the reasons I have just given, such as advertising and merchandising, but the sugarfree products have experienced a dramatic increase in sales.

There is only one reason for this phenomenon, and that is the quality of our Orbit sugarfree product. When the product was relaunched with Nutrasweet, it was not advertised or promoted in any way whatsoever, but it was the consumer who over a period of time realised this was an excellent product. In fact, it is unique to the chewing gum market that a sugarfree product, in some cases, can have a superior taste and a much longer lasting flavour than its sugar counterpart.

As a result of a much improved and superior quality product, the increase in sales is coming not only from existing consumers who are consuming more product, but more importantly from completely new consumers to the category who are accounting for over 50% of all new sales today.

In addition to Orbit sugarfree, we have this year introduced another product which is a sugarfree coated pellet product called Wrigley's Extra, which uses xylitol as its main coating ingredient and is an outstanding product in the confectionery market. However, because xylitol is an expensive ingredient, the product has to be sold at a premium which, from the results so far, consumers are prepared to pay for.

These two products combined are the reason why 32% of our business next year will be accounted for by sugarfree products, and we anticipate that this growth will continue into the future. We still believe that consumers will buy sucrose sweetened products because they like the

98

particular taste, texture and flavour, but an increasing proportion of
consumers will turn to sugarfree products and an increasing number of new
consumers will enter the market specifically for sugarfree products.
Consumers buy sugarfree chewing gum for a variety of reasons. Generally
speaking it is to avoid an intake of sugar and because they want to reduce
the number of calories that they are consuming. In the case of chewing
gum, the total number of calories per stick is very small compared to the
average confectionery product. However, there is a general trend toward a
healthier lifestyle, healthier eating and the avoidance of certain
ingredients such as saturated fats, sodium and sugar which can have a
detrimental affect one one's health and on one's teeth. In the case of
sugar-based chewing gum the evidence is somewhat different since the
little sucrose in the gum is chewed out within the first two or three
minutes and the consumer then finds himself with basically what is a sugar-
free gum.

Most meals and snacks contain fermentable carbohydrates which can
cause acid attacks, and the increase in the habit of snacking can lead to
frequent and prolonged acid attacks on one's teeth.

Whether it is a sugar gum or a sugarfree gum, the effect of chewing
as we all know is to stimulate saliva which in turn neutralises the plaque
acids in the mouth in a period of less than 20 minutes of gum chewing. In
addition, there is some evidence from recent studies that the abundance of
saliva will actually help to remineralise whitespot lesions if one chews
after every meal or snack. Wrigley's chewing gums do not have any active
ingredients that promote good dental health in themselves; it is Mother
Nature's own saliva which is the active ingredient, and the abundance is
the result of the chewing action. This, in fact, forms our basis for
promoting good dental health, as an adjunct to regular brushing, use of
fluoride toothpaste and flossing, in that we recommend that after you eat
you shouldn't forget to chew. This is a copy of an advertisement which
appeared in the national daily press at the end of last year. Those of
you who have read it will remember that no specific claims were made for
chewing gum per se, but the benefits from saliva were the main thrust of
the text of the advertisement. Whilst we are awaiting further research
for sucrose sweetened gum, we believe this is a responsible approach in
the context of the present attitudes towards sugar by the profession.

SUMMARY

To summarise my last section, I have tried to demonstrate that
reformulation can have a dramatic effect on a product's acceptance by the
consuming public on condition that it produces an excellent quality and
can even attract new users to the category. At the same time, chewing gum
which is one of the most widely available confectionery products in the
U.K. has potentially an important role to play in dental health by helping
to neutralise the plaque acid attacks caused by frequent snacking in
today's diet as well as helping to remineralise early white spot lesions.

In conclusion, I have tried to demonstrate the composition of the
U.K. confectionery market, and that the per-capita consumption has not
increased dramatically, even though the way confectionery is consumed has
changed. I have demonstrated the complexity with which the confectionery
industry is confronted with the different types of sugarfree ingredients
and their limitations, and I have shown that if one is able to produce a
first class quality product, the consuming public will beat your door down
to obtain it. At the same time, I have demonstrated that chewing gum can
have a role to play in the context of good dental health as well.

SUGARS, SWEETENERS AND EC REGULATIONS

PIERRE-MARIE VINCENT
French Food Law Association
''Folle Avoine'', Le Brulat
83330 Le Castellet, France

ABSTRACT

Sucrose, sugars and sweeteners are governed by regulations at national and EC level.

These regulations give definitions of products, fix their uses and use levels, and also deal with labelling, declarations and claims.

There are discrepancies from one country to another and, at EC level, some uncertainties remain. Some important points, regarding mainly health claims, have to be discussed before final regulations will be issued.

INTRODUCTION

There are very evident scientific differences between sugars and sweeteners, chemically, physically and biologically.

At public perception level, things are very confused due to insufficient knowledge on one side and somewhat misinformed advertising on the other. It is hoped that regulations, those brass-engraved Tables of the Law issued by highly responsible governments, will clear up this situation.

Laws, however, are the living image of man and are thus variable and inaccurate. They change from country to country and also over a period of time.

We have to live with them, however, and the aim of this paper will be to describe those regulations governing the subjects of this Symposium, namely sugars and sweeteners in Europe.

LEGAL DEFINITIONS

As already mentioned in the introduction, these definitions are in some cases, not always scientifically correct. These examples will be underlined for convenience.

Laws generally make a distinction between sugar, sugars and the (modern) sugar substitutes, and include honey in this large group of 'sweetening agents'.

Sugar

The word sugar is officially defined in an EC directive and it is equivalent to sucrose or, in other words, the product obtained from sugar beet and/or sugar cane. This definition is widely accepted.

Sugars

At EC level, this term embodies sugar per se and the other sweetening substances with chemical formulae near to the sucrose molecule, such as glucose and fructose.

The glucose family

Glucose is the basic sugar circulating in the human body and in plant sap. Pure glucose is called dextrose. The glucose syrup group also includes the isomerized glucose syrups. All these products of the glucose family are made from starch and this is why, in the US, glucose syrup is called corn syrup.

Invert sugar

When sucrose is hydrolysed, a mixture of fructose and dextrose is obtained. Rather strangely, invert sugar is legally considered to be 'sugar'.

Fructose

This is also called fruit sugar and is now manufactured from sugar or hydrolized starch. Fructose is not legally defined in all countries but when defined, the definition generally covers only pure fructose (also called laevulose) and not the syrups very rich in this product.

Maltose

This is also called malt sugar. It is not widely used as such but is an important component of glucose syrups. As with fructose, maltose is not legally defined in all countries.

Lactose

This is also called milk sugar and is the main sweetening agent in milk. As in previous examples, lactose is not legally defined in all countries.

Sugar substitutes

Here there are legal complications.

In most countries, this expression covered and still covers everything with a sweet taste which does not belong to the 'sugars' family. In the past, official bodies in some countries tried to include, under this collective name, all non-sucrose sweeteners.

It is now generally accepted that sugar substitutes are: the polyols, polydextrose and the intense sweeteners.

In the FRG, fructose is also considered as a sugar substitute.

Sweeteners

This is the new word used by the EEC to (legally) define the non-sugar sweetening agents. It more or less replaces the term sugar substitutes.

The Germans will have difficulties to legally translate this term since, for them, Sussstoffe (=sweeteners) are the so-called intense sweeteners...

Under this kind of vocabulary pressure, the EEC made a distinction between 'bulk sweeteners', i.e. polyols and polydextrose, and 'intense sweeteners'.

Polyols

Polyols are 'bulk sweeteners'. They have some calorific value (the exact values are another dispute) and they are bulky in the sense of having a given volume.

One can make hard candies only with polyols, for example.

Some polyols occur naturally in plants (sorbitol, mannitol, xylitol), but all are now made industrially by hydrogenation of sugars (glucose gives sorbitol, maltose maltitol, fructose mannitol, xylose xylitol and lactose lactitol, to give some examples).

The legally permitted polyols are:

- sorbitol and its syrups
- mannitol
- maltitol and its syrups
- xylitol
- lactitol
- isomalt

Polydextrose

This is a separate case. Polydextrose (a polymer of dextrose) is certainly not a polyol, but is often legally considered in the same class.

Polydextrose has a low sweet taste, but good bulking properties. Its calorific value is accepted to be lower than those of the polyols.

Intense sweeteners

For once, the legal term is perfectly descriptive. It adequately replaces the term 'artificial sweeteners' previously used.

At their levels of use intense sweeteners have no calorific value and have a sweetening power far greater than those of sugars and polyols.

If the sweetening power of sucrose is 1, glucose is 0.7, fructose 1.3, sorbitol 0.6, whereas cyclamate has 30, saccharin 300, ...

Owing to their very low use rates, intense sweeteners impart no bulking effect.

The legally permitted intense sweeteners are:

- Acesulfame potassium

- Aspartame

- cyclamic acid and its Na and Ca salts

- saccharin and its Na, K and Ca salts

- Thaumatin

- neo-hesperidin dihydrochalcone

with two additions which may be permitted in the near future:

- Sucralose.

- Alitame

Honey

Since manna (and especially ash-tree manna) is no longer
consumed today, the only ready-to-eat natural sweetener
is honey.

The word 'honey' brings with it its historical and
gastronomical flavor, but also its very strict legal
definition. Most, if not all countries, have given honey
a legal status. Switzerland has even a legal definition
of 'artificial honey' (Kunsthonig), a product generally
known as golden syrup.

LEGISLATION: a foreword

What are the main purposes (or reasons) for regulations
and, especially in our case, for food regulations?
First of all, they protect the consumer's health.
Regulated foods are either well known or duly tested for
their absolute or relative safety before being approved
and listed. They can be considered as food ingredients
or as food additives.
Food regulations also define, or try to define, the
regulated product. This definition is, of course,
closely related to safety and refers to the degree of
purity, thus enabling control analysis.
Food regulations not only define the product, but permit
its use.

In many countries, specified rules are needed before putting a food product on the market or mixing it with others. Even today, and as an example, the use of glucose is not allowed in France in most dairy products where sucrose is normally used.

Use permission goes very often with use levels and even sucrose cannot be, to give another example, used without limit in marmalade, where fruit and sugar levels are fixed by law.

Food regulations protect and inform the consumer through labelling.

In the framework of this Symposium, it is important to note that claims and especially health-claims are legally regulated, some being even strictly prohibited.

GENERAL LEGISLATION AT EC LEVEL

At the present time, some sweetening agents are bound by EC common rules, some others will soon be included.

Some are not, however, leaving the use of the product to national regulations which may of course differ from country to country. If a product is legally approved in one EC country it can be sold in the others. Sold, but not manufactured, and the European Court of Justice is looking at ambiguous cases, of which there are many.

The 'Certain Sugars Directive'

In the impossibility of regulating all 'sugars', i.e. mainly the mono- and disaccharides, the EC issued, in the 'Official Journal of the European Communities, December 73, a Directive governing 'certain' sugars. Included herein are:

- the various types of sucrose
- invert sugar
- the various types of glucose and dextrose, including isomerized glucose syrups.

All these products are recognized as food ingredients. The directive gives only definitions and purity criteria.

The 'non-regulated sugars'

As mentioned before, they are:

- fructose
- lactose
- maltose

These three products are generally recognized as food ingredients.

'Sugar substitutes' in the forthcoming EC-regulations

For reasons not always easy to understand, the EC Commission considers all these sugar substitutes, today called 'sweeteners' as food additives. There were, for years, hard discussions to try to give, at least to some of them (polyols for instance) the valorizing status of food ingredients. The proposed directive 'on sweeteners for use in foodstuffs' (actual document Nr. III/3597/90) can be regarded as a compromise.

This directive on sweeteners will form a part of the big frame-directive 89/107 of 21 December 1988 on food additives. It will provide:

- a list of sweeteners the use of which is authorized to the exclusion of all others,

- the list of foodstuffs to which these sweeteners may be added, the conditions under which they may be added and, where appropriate, a limit on the technological purpose of their use.

Specifications of identity and purity will come later. According to the text, the term 'sugar-free' will mean 'without any added mono- and disaccharides', forgetting that glucose syrups contain a certain amount of tri- and polysaccharides...

111

Six polyols are included (sorbitol and sorbitol syrups, mannitol, xylitol, maltitol and maltitol syrup, isomalt and lactitol) and provided with E numbers.

They can be used without limit ('quantum satis') in 'all foodstuffs excluding water-based flavoured non-alcoholic drinks'.

Looked at through dentists' eyes, it says that polyols can be used to manufacture 'sugarfree' candies and other confectionery products which can be considered as useful for caries prevention.

The intense sweeteners listed are:

- Acesulfame K (E 950)

- Aspartame (E 951)

- cyclamic acid and its Na and Ca salts (E 952)

- saccharin and its Na, K and Ca salts (E 954)

- Thaumatin (E 957)

- neo-hesperidine DC (E 959)

Some E numbers are missing and there is space available for other intense sweeteners (like Sucralose for instance whose toxicological status is already under discussion at international level).

The other point worth mentioning is that all the listed intense sweeteners are generally intended for use in 'energy reduced or sugar-free' foodstuffs, some of them being also approved for use in 'special diets'.

Polydextrose is no longer considered either as a sugar substitute or as a sweetener. It is found now, under E 1200, in a list of 'Generally Permitted Food Additives' in a forthcoming specific directive (working document III/9049/90) covering 'certain food additives' and being issued within the frame of the so-called comprehensive Directive 89/107.

This concept of Generally Permitted Food Additives is new at EEC level, although somewhat similar to the Miscellaneous Additives in the UK (and to the GRAS products in the USA).

Looking at these drafts, one may raise some questions. The first one is whether some 'sweeteners' (namely polyols) are really food additives when they are used in full substitution of sugars, in hard candies for instance. A food additive is, by definition, something added to something else. In the case of a hard-boiled candy made of 99 % of polyols, the rest being colours and flavours, the question remains open.

The second question, related to the first one but of a more general nature, is whether sweetness is a technological function.

By progressing this way of thinking, salt and pepper may soon also be food additives.

And by going even further, we arrive at the Swedish legal situation where sucrose is a food additive with a specific S number.

Honey is regulated, at EC level, by a directive, number 74/409 dated July 22nd, 1974. The Greeks at that time were not members of the EEC.

THE GENERAL REGULATIONS IN EUROPEAN COUNTRIES

The 'sugars'

As previously stated, most 'sugars' are governed by the EC Directive on certain sugars, but others have a status varying from country to country.

Fructose (with a sweetening power higher than that of sucrose) is very often permitted in dietetic foods (diabetics, infant foods, foods for athletes,...).

Energy reduced foods may, in France, contain fructose.

In Belgium, Spain, Denmark, Italy, UK and Greece, fructose is an ordinary sugar.

The 'sweeteners'

In expectation of the forthcoming specific directive, regulations at present vary from country to country, hindering the free movement of foodstuffs.

The table at the end of this paper (kindly provided by Roquette Frères) gives an idea of the discrepancies as far as polyols and polydextrose are concerned today.

Similar tables may be produced for intense sweeteners, showing even larger discrepancies due to the more controversial attitude of the national health authorities regarding the safety status of these products.

SPECIFIC REGULATIONS AND RELATED CLAIMS

To market a foodstuff, the manufacturer has to advertise it, and to advertise it, he has to (or at least may) write something on the label or on the related advertising (newspaper, radio, TV, etc...).

Declarations and claims are supposed to reflect and underline the qualitites and advantages of the foodstuff in question, and are related to present day attitudes of the consumer.

In recent years, consumers are becoming more and more health-oriented and thus the manufacturers and their respective Marketing Departments have developed declarations like 'sugarfree', 'sugarless', 'light', 'no-calories', 'reduced-calories', and so on.

As a result of this health wave, it was obvious that the Authorities at national and EC level (and also the US, Canadian or Japanese authorities which have the same attitude) to control this wave by regulating these advertisements and by issuing so-called 'mandatory labelling'. One is already foreseen regarding 'sugar-free' and, most probably, further will come.

It is generally admitted that these kinds of declaration have only a partial relation to health, and no relation whatsoever with human disease.

Some others are directly health-related and constitute real claims.

To avoid unrealistic, unscientifically based claims, national authorities have issued strict regulations. EC health authorities are preparing even stricter regulations, the latest being a draft of a directive (document 111/8300/89) covering what was called declarations and claims. The idea behind this was that health related claims can only be used when they are not dealing with human disease. In other words, how far a food manufacturer may proceed with such claims, or where the border line exists between human health and human disease.

Along with this double question is another one: is food able to cure disease?

The answer to this last question is no, witness the exact title of the EC directive governing what people call dietetic products: 'foodstuffs intended for particular nutritional uses'. The title speaks about nutrition, and not about diseases or organs and shows that nutrition is only a part of the general cure of disease. The list of groups of foods foreseen in this directive is a good indication of the sense of this statement.

The answer to the first two questions, however, is still pending. Health and regulatory authorities are trying to take firm and scientifically based positions, with the food manufacturer trying to get the best possible marketing advantages.

The first clear point is that no mention whatsoever of a human disease shall be put in the advertising and/or the claim, what is fully in line with the previous question. Food alone does not cure disease, it may just contribute to re-establish an unbalanced situation (deficiencies in vitamins, in mineral salts, in essential fatty acids, or, the reverse : excess of fat, carbohydrates and so on).

This symposium being devoted to dental health, it is not the intention of the author to discuss diabetes or cardio-vascular disease, but rather to concentrate on caries, thus leading to other questions:

-    Is caries a disease (from which someone may die)?

-    Are sugarless products able to cure caries?

The medical/scientific aspects having been already discussed here, the only pending point is the regulatory one, i.e. the possible claims, which should be truthful, accurate and not misleading.

They already exist (physically and legally) in various European countries and in the US as:

- does not promote tooth decay
- kinder to teeth
- toothfriendly
- zahnschonend
- zahnfreundlich
- menage les dents

Since these claims do not imply any therapeutic or mitigating effect on a disease (dental caries), they are not considered as drug claims. But, under the provisions of the draft of the Directive on Claims, they may no longer be permitted, and such a development would be a step backwards in terms of consumer information.

The German authorities, backed by their own very strict regulations, were of the same opinion as that expressed in this draft of directive. But, after thorough discussions, they finally accepted the word 'toothfriendly' (= zahnfreundlich).

No doubt the EC authorities will be convinced by the arguments laid down in Germany, with the help of the COMA

Report No. 37, 'Dietary Sugars and Human Disease'
already cited.

It is perfectly clear that no mention of caries shall
appear on the claim. It is clear also that, according to
the people of the Faculty for Dental Medicine of Zurich
University, the consumption of 'sugarless' foodstuffs
contributes to the general prevention of caries.

To substantiate a claim, we need a clear definition of
the products bearing it, and a method of control. These
two elements have already been submitted to the EC
authorities (and are very similar to the article 185i of
the Swiss Food Ordinance).

They are:

- the foodstuff shall not contain any sugar(s) or
  other fermentable carbohydrates
- the foodstuffs are confirmed to lack cariogenic
  potential by expert opinion based on appropriate,
  well-conducted in vivo tests

In our opinion, the claims 'does not promote tooth
decay' or 'kinder for teeth' or 'toothfriendly' should
go on the label, with the declaration 'sugarless' or
'sugar-free' so that the consumer can be fully aware of
the situation (if he reads and understands the label).

CONCLUSIONS

As one may see, regulations are a complex (and somewhat hard to understand) matter.

As long as they remain of general order, they are more or less easy to live with, but problems arise when they try to go into detail, and especially when they introduce science and more especially human biology which is always a very controversial matter. Philosophy is also very controversial but is, in this case, an opportunity to conclude by recalling what was said in the introduction. Laws are the living image of man and it depends upon you to decide what kind of man you would like to be.

POLYOLS - FOOD LEGAL STATUS

	GERMANY	BELGIUM	DENMARK	FRANCE	HOLLAND	ITALY
POLYDEXTROSE	–	*(2)	–	*(12)	–	–
LYCASIN 80/55	°(1)	*	*(6)	*(12)	*	*(13)
SORBITOL	*	*	*(6)	*(12)	*	70% (14)
MANNITOL	*(1)	*(3)	*(6)	*(12)	*	10% (14)
XYLITOL	*	*	*(6)	*(12)	*	*(13)
ISOMALT	°(1)	°(4)	special permit	*(12)	*	–
MALTITOL	°(1)	*	*(6)	*(12)	*	*(13)
LACTITOL	–	*(5)	–	*(12)	*	–

	UK	SWEDEN	SWITZER- LAND	AUSTRIA	USA	FAO OMS
POLYDEXTROSE	*(15)	*(17)	*(19)	–	*	*(7)
LYCASIN 80/55	*	*	*	*	*	*(8)
SORBITOL	*	*	*	*	*	*(9)
MANNITOL	*	*	*	5%	*	*(10)
XYLITOL	*	*	*	*	*	*(11)
ISOMALT	*	+(18)	*	–	–	*(8)
MALTITOL	*(16)	*	*	*(16)	*	*(20)
LACTITOL	*	–	*(20)	–	–	*(11)

* : Approved

– : Forbidden

+ : Tolerated

° : New draft regulation with a favourable outcome

N O T E S

(1) A modification of the German food additives regulations
     intends to:

     - authorize LYCASIN 80/55 and ISOLMALT according to
       GMP in confections, chewing-gum, marzipan and
       similar products, nougat products

     - authorize ISOMALT according to GMP in table top
       products dietetic products, chewing-gum, soft and
       hard caramel and 10% in other foodstuffs

     For the time being, an 'Ausnahmegenehmigung' (special
     permission) is necessary.

(2) Only in reduced-energy foodstuffs (A.R. 30/6/89)

(3) GMP in chewing-gum (A.R. 30/6/89) and in flavouring
     substances

(4) A modification of the Belgium food additives regulations
     intends to authorize ISOMALT according to GMP in
     confectionery, bakery products (only in reduced-energy
     bakery products), chocolates (only in filled chocolate
     products)

(5) According to A.R. 30/6/89, LACTITOL is permitted
according to GMP in reduced-energy ice-cream and
their preparations reduced-energy marzipan,
reduced-energy bakery products.

(6) GMP in chewing-gum and throat pastilles, 10% in other
confectionery products

(7) 25th JECFA (1981) ADI: 0-70 mg/kg

(8) 29th JECFA (1985) ADI: not specifified

(9) 26th JECFA (1982) ADI: not specifified

(10) 30th JECFA (1986) ADI: not specificied
report not yet published

(11) 27th JECFA (1983) ADI: not specified

(12) A declaration must be made to the 'Prefecture du
Departement', a polyol based product being a dietetic
product

(13) Special demand (dietetic regulation)

(14) Only in chewing-gum. For other products, a petition
file must be submitted.

(15) Miscellaneous additives in food

(16) Hydrogenated glucose syrup containing 90% maltitol

(17) 15% in ice-cream

(18) If the level exceeds 15%, the following information
shall be given on the container: 'this product contains
isomalt (xg/100 g) which may have a laxative effect'.

(19) POLYDEXTROSE is considered as a bulking agent and
not as a sweetener. Its legal status is under
examination at the 'Office Federal de la Sante'.
In the meantime, authorization is given by local
administration ('chimistes cantonnaux').

(20) Circulaire no. 20 du 11/10/89.
Ne peut-etre employe que pour l'edulcoration des
aliments dietetiques et speciaux.

Val. Cal.: 2 Kcal/g.

'Peut avoir un effect laxatif' si le produit contient
plus de 10 g de Lactitol.

SUGARS AND DENTAL HEALTH IN YOUNG CHILDREN

PAMELA HOBSON
Department of Oral Health and Development,
University of Manchester Dental School,
Higher Cambridge Street, Manchester M15 6FH.

ABSTRACT

Dental caries is one of the most common diseases affecting children. The effects of the disease and its treatment on otherwise healthy children are considerable. Additional problems occur in children who are handicapped, while in those with a wide range of chronic medical disorders there may be an associated serious risk to general health. The levels of the disease are unacceptably high and the treatment is costly. Evidence indicates that intake of sugar is the most important dietary factor in the aetiology of dental caries and to prevent the disease it is necessary to control its consumption. In some sick children whose general health is at risk in the presence of dental disease, development of caries is associated with use of sugar-containing paediatric medicines. Action taken to overcome this problem has resulted in limited success.

INTRODUCTION

The disease which occurs commonly in the mouths of children is dental caries, this leads to pain and loss of teeth. It is necessary to consider its effects on children, the aetiology of the disease and the method of prevention; the appropriate steps can then be taken to promote dental health in childhood. Disease free mouths in young children provide an excellent foundation for ongoing dental health thus enabling people to maintain their teeth throughout life.

SIGNIFICANCE OF DENTAL CARIES

Healthy Children

Dental caries in otherwise healthy children causes a number of problems.
If the disease is treated in its early stages, fillings can be inserted under
local analgesia and, if correctly handled, most children are able to accept
this procedure. However, there are some children who are unable to
accept treatment, particularly the very young and those with emotional
problems. If treatment is not provided the disease progresses and pain
develops. In many cases the child's appearance is also affected. Some
young children develop a condition termed "bottle caries" which occurs
when a feeding bottle containing a sweetened drink is used over
prolonged periods. This frequently occurs when the child goes to bed
with a feeding bottle as a comforter. The action of the drink flowing over
the teeth causes a rapid development of dental caries and leads to
toothache (1).

Extensive dental caries in children in any age group is frequently
associated with severe pain, and dental abscesses may occur with facial
swelling. This commonly leads to sleepless nights for both the child and
his parents. At this stage extraction is generally unavoidable, and in
young patients the administration of a general anaesthetic is usually
required. In the past this operation was commonly performed in the dental
surgery. However, although it is in general a safe procedure, it must be
taken seriously because some children develop problems while they are
anaesthetised. Sadly, in a number of these cases the child has died.
Because of the risks associated with general anaesthesia in young children,
many authorities now consider that it should always be administered in
hospital, so that the necessary resuscitative skills and equipment are
immediately available. The admission into hospital of all children who
require dental extractions under general anaesthetic would be extremely
costly and would put an additional load onto the already over-stretched
hospital service.

There are other problems associated with dental extractions in
children. The whole procedure is worrying for the parents and can be
very frightening for a child, often making them reluctant to accept dental
care in the future. If many teeth are lost the child may have difficulty in
eating, and soft foodstuffs are chosen rather than those which provide the

appropriate nutrients. In some cases early loss of the deciduous or first teeth allows the permanent teeth to drift from their correct position, leading to the need for expensive and time consuming orthodontic treatment when the child is older.

Handicapped Children

Presence of dental caries can create additional difficulties in children with a physical or mental handicap. In children who are physically handicapped it may be impossible for them to get to the dental surgery for care without the use of an ambulance, and access to the surgery can be difficult for those in wheelchairs. In children with a severe mental handicap, lack of co-operation makes dental treatment extremely difficult. In some cases administration of a general anaesthetic in hospital is required even before an examination of the mouth can be carried out and, subsequently, general anaesthesia is necessary whenever treatment is needed. This is a cause for serious concern because of the associated risk to general health, particularly if the child has active dental caries and treatment under general anaesthesia is required on a regular basis. In addition to the risks involved, procedures of this type are extremely costly in terms of facilities, money and staff time.

Chronically Sick Children

There is another group of children who suffer from a wide range of medical disorders in whom presence of dental disease and sepsis or dental treat-ment procedures put the general health or even the life of the child in jeopardy. For example, those with cardiac, respiratory or kidney disease; haematological disorders such as haemophilia; neoplastic disease, including leukaemia; disorders of the immune system and patients who have received cardiac, renal or bone marrow transplants (2). For all these children who are medically compromised in the dental situation, presence of dental caries and need for treatment can have grave consequences and lead to an increase in morbidity. Paediatricians now consider that prevention of dental disease in these patients is an important part of their general health care and every effort should be made to ensure that dental caries does not develop.

Social Problems

Dental disease also affects the child's family unit. When a young patient is required to visit the dentist for a prolonged course of treatment the parent has to accompany the child to the surgery. This can be difficult if there are many young children in the family, when there are social problems or when both parents are working. It is particularly difficult for the one parent family where the need to have time off work may jeopardise the parent's job. In parents with these problems, dental health assumes a low priority and, quite understandably, they are often unable to attend the dentist for routine care to be provided for their child. Caries then progresses untreated until pain develops and extraction is unavoidable.

EXTENT OF THE PROBLEM

A study into the dental health of children in the U.K. showed that levels of dental caries differed in different parts of the country. As these data (3) are presented as average figures, some of the children included were caries free and others had very extensive disease. The average number of carious teeth in 5 year old children was lowest in England (1.6) and highest in Northern Ireland (3.7). A similar pattern occurred in 12 year old children where again the average was lowest in England (2.9) and highest in Northern Ireland (4.8). Within England there was also a wide variation in the disease levels in different Regions, with those in the north being markedly more severally affected than those in the south. There was also a considerable variation associated with social class, with the socially disadvantaged having the most extensive dental disease. For example, in 5 year olds from social classes I, II and III the average number of carious teeth was 1.3 compared to 2.6 in children from social classes IV and V. There was a similar situation in the 12 year old group where the average number of carious teeth ranged from 2.8 in social classes I, II and III to 3.3 in social classes IV and V. This effect of social class on levels of health is reflected in many statistics of health levels in childhood such as respiratory disease and infant mortality (4).

Data of the treatment provided for young children in the General Dental Service in England and Wales and the high cost of that treatment is of interest (5). These data give no indication of the disease levels because it omits the many carious teeth which remain untreated, and it does not include treatment provided in the Community and Hospital Dental Services or treatment provided privately. The number of fillings placed in deciduous teeth in a year in the G.D.S. amounted to over 1,770,000, and this cost the N.H.S. over £9,077,000. The number of extracted deciduous teeth was 1,010,000 costing £3,680,000. The majority of these teeth would have been extracted following the administration of a general anaesthetic. During the same period 250,000 general anaesthetics were administered in England and Wales to children aged 0-14 years, the cost of this treatment was £2,990,000. These examples give some indication of the amounts of money which the N.H.S. is required to spend in treating dental disease in young children. However, the most unfortunate aspect of this situation is the mortality rate of children undergoing extraction of teeth under general anaesthesia. For example, in the North Western Region of England at least four children have died in this way in the last six years (6).

AETIOLOGY AND PREVENTION

The aetiology of dental caries is complex, but epidemiological, clinical and animal research has lead to a greater understanding of the process (7). It is now generally agreed that it is initiated by an acid attack on the tooth. Bacteria which are present in the mouth metabolise sugar, which is consumed in foods and drinks, to form acid which breaks down the thin outer enamel layer and allows the disease to progress through the tooth until the infection reaches the dental pulp. This leads to pain and abscess development.

An important method of preventing the disease is to control the acid attack which initiates it. The recently published COMA Report (8) reviewed the extensive scientific evidence on this subject. It reported:-

"The Panel found no evidence that the consumption of most sugars naturally incorporated in the cellular structure of foods (intrinsic sugars) represented a threat to health"

Intrinsic sugars are those which occur naturally within the cells of foods such as fresh fruit and vegetables. The COMA Report went on to review the evidence relating to the intake of those sugars which are NOT incorporated into the cellular structure of foods, the so called "extrinsic sugars". These processed products include glucose, fructose and sucrose, with sucrose being the sugar most commonly used in the U.K. Referring to these extrinsic sugars the report concluded:-

"Extensive evidence suggests that sugars are the most important dietary factor in the cause of dental caries".

Sugar is included in many foods and drinks for example, biscuits, cakes, ice cream, jam, fruit cordials, carbonated drinks or pop and many people add sugar to tea and coffee. It is also present in many less obvious processed foods, these are known as the "hidden sugars". For example, it is present in sauces, ketchups, breakfast cereals, tinned soups and tinned vegetables. Sugar is also included in numerous medicinal products such as antibiotics, cough medicines and lozenges, and in many medicines prepared especially for use by children.

In view of the overwhelming evidence that use of sugar is the most important dietary factor in the cause of the disease, the COMA Report recommended that, in order to reduce the risk of dental caries, the consumption of sugar by the population should be decreased and that it should be replaced by fresh fruit, vegetables and starchy foods. It also recommended that there should be a reduction in the consumption of sugary snacks.

The report acknowledged that caries risk can be reduced by non dietary means, particularly by use of fluoride, but it stressed that these methods offer incomplete protection and some are expensive to implement.

PROBLEMS ASSOCIATED WITH PAEDIATRIC MEDICINES

The pharmaceutical industry prepares special medicines for use by children. The medication is frequently presented in liquid form because children may be unable to take tablets or capsules, and because it is easy to adjust the dose of a liquid to make it suitable for a small child. In order to make medicines palatable for these young patients, sugar has been incorporated as a sweetener for many years. Other advantages of sugar are that it is cheap, it acts as a preservative and is a bulking agent which gives the product the required viscosity (9).

In 1984 an examination of the various medicines formulated for both adults and children revealed that over 60% of the preparations contained sugar, but the proportion of special preparations for children which contained sugar reached almost 100% (10). Until recently when standard medicines required to be diluted for children, the British National Formulary and the British Pharmocopoeia recommended that syrup should be used as the diluent (11).

As long ago as 1953 it was suggested that use of syrupy medicines damaged teeth (12). Subsequently, the problem has been clearly demonstrated in a clinical study (13). This used two groups of matched children aged under six years. The test group had been taking sugar-based medicines regularly for at least six months and when compared with the control group, who had not received sweetened medications, it was found that the test group had a significantly higher caries experience. The conclusion was drawn that long-term administration of medicines sweetened with sugar was associated with an increase in dental caries in children. This condition has been termed "medication caries" (14).

There has been reluctance on the part of the pharmaceutical industry to respond to this problem and to omit sugar from medicines for children. This requires the need to use an alternative sweetener/flavouring agent to mask the taste of the drug and use of additional constituents to provide the other required properties. The product must then be tested and licensed. This whole procedure is time consuming and expensive. For some time a more satisfactory situation has existed in some other countries. For example in Sweden, where a wide variety of sugar-free liquid medicines, including antibiotics and cough medicines has been available; these have been widely prescribed by paediatricians.

There has been concern about the lack of progress over this matter in the U.K., and in 1985 joint action was taken by six professional organisations including dentists, paediatricians and pharmacists. These organisations acted as a pressure group which contacted the DHSS expressing concern about the situation (15). This lead to some improvement. The Medicines Control Agency of the Department of Health is now aware of the cariogenic effect of sugar-containing medicines in children. Pharmaceutical companies making applications for product licenses are frequently requested to undertake reformulation to remove sugar from paediatric medicines, particularly when products are intended for long term use.

Action has also been taken by the British National Formulary which marks liquid preparations which are free of cariogenic sugar as "sugar free". Furthermore, the British Pharmocopoeia no longer

recommends syrups be used as diluents for liquid preparations. A measure
of the improvement has been shown in the published lists of all
sugar-free preparations (for adults and children). These show that the
numbers have increased from 106 sugar-free medicines in 1985 (16) to
235 in 1988 (17).

Unfortunately, however, a considerable number of liquid preparations
such as antibiotics which may be prescribed for children on a long-term
basis are still only available in a sugar vehicle. Another example is
digoxin elixir which is prescribed for young children with heart defects.
Although digoxin tablets can be prescribed for the older child there is, at
present, no suitable alternative to the sugar containing elixir for younger
children, other than an unlicensed preparation which the manufacturers
can only supply on request on a named patient basis (18). It is highly
unsatisfactory that this valuable medicine is not more readily available in
a sugar-free form and it is a particular cause for concern because in
children with heart disease there is severe morbidity associated with dental
disease.

CONCLUSION

It has been shown that there is extensive scientific evidence to indicate
that consumption of the so called "extrinsic sugars" such as sucrose leads
to the development of dental caries. It causes much pain, disfigurement
and tooth loss in our children, and it is also extremely costly to treat.
Furthermore, in some children the disease can put their health, or even
their life at risk. In the main it is this group of sick children who require
the prolonged treatment with medicines which have been shown to cause
dent l disease. As this disease can be prevented in our young children by
the control of sugar intake, it is the responsibility of all those involved to
take steps to ensure that this is done.

REFERENCES

1. Winter, G.B., Hamilton, M.C., and James, P.M.C., Role of the
   comforter as an aetiological factor in rampant caries in the deciduous
   dentition. Arch. Dis. Childh., 1966, 41, 207-12.

2.   Hobson, P., The treatment of medically handicapped children. Int. Dent. J., 1980, 30, 6–13.

3.   Todd, J.E. and Dodd, T., Children's dental health in the United Kingdom 1983. Office of Population Censuses and Surveys, Social Survey Division, H.M.S.O., London, 1985.

4.   Fit for the future. The Report of the Committee on Child Health Services. Department of Health and Social Security, H.M.S.O., London, 1976.

5.   Digest of Statistics, 1987–88. The Dental Estimates Board for England and Wales.

6.   Personal communication.

7.   Rugg-Gunn, A.J., Diet and dental caries. In The Prevention of Dental Disease, ed. J.J. Murray, Oxford University Press, Oxford, 1989, pp. 4–114.

8.   Dietary sugars and human disease. Report of the Panel on Dietary sugars, Committee on Medical Aspects of Food Policy, Department of Health, H.M.S.O., London, 1989.

9.   Hobson, P., Sugar based medicines and dental disease. Community Dent. Hlth., 2, 57–62.

10. National Pharmaceutical Association. Sugar content of medicines. The National Pharmaceutical Association, St. Albans, 1984.

11. British National Formulary. London, British Medical Association and The Pharmaceutical Society of Great Britain.

12. James, P.M.C. and Parfitt, G.F., Local effects of certain medicaments on the teeth. Br. Med. J., 1953, 2, 1252–53.

13. Roberts, I.F. and Roberts, G.J. Relations between medicines sweetened with sucrose and dental disease. Br. Med. J., 1979, 2, 14–16.

14. Hobson, P., Dietary control and prevention of dental disease in chronically sick children. J. Hum. Nutr., 1979, 33, 140–45.

15. Hobson, P. and Fuller, S., Sugar based medicines and dental disease – progress report. Community Dent. Hlth., 4, 169–76.

16. Brandon, M. and Sadler, E.B., Sugar-free medicines. Pharmaceut. J. 1985, 234, 824.

17. Sadler, E.B. and Brandon, M., Update on sugar-free medicines. Pharmaceut. J. 1988, 241, 16–17.

18. Personal communication.

A SURVEY OF THE USE OF LIQUID ORAL MEDICINES

ANNE MAGUIRE
Department of Child Dental Health,
University of Newcastle Upon Tyne,
United Kingdom.

ABSTRACT

The use of long-term liquid oral medication by children aged
1-16 years of age in a number of districts within the
Northern Region was surveyed. Fifty eight different liquid
oral preparations were taken daily by 190 children for
periods longer than three months at the time of the study.
This represented a prevalence of 0.09% or 1:1100 children
between the ages of 1-16 years in the five districts
studied. The most common preparation taken long-term was
the anti-convulsant agent sodium valproate. There was a
wide age distribution in children taking liquid medication
with 40% below the age of 5 years and 43% aged 5-11 years.
Thirty three percent of the liquid medicines used long term
were sugar-based, 31% sugar-free and 36% either sugar-based
or sugar-free (variable) depending upon the specificity of
the prescribing. The increasing use of generic preparations
in prescribing and dispensing was highlighted, together with
a recommendation that manufacturers of liquid generic
preparations should be encouraged to provide suitable sugar-
free alternatives.

INTRODUCTION

In the treatment of child and adult patients, the medical
and dental professions often have a difficult task ensuring
the compliance of the patient to a particular medication
regime.

The use of pleasant-tasting syrupy liquids has helped
in the administration of these drugs to child and geriatric
patients for decades. However it has been postulated that
the use of sugar-containing liquid oral medicines poses a

potential threat to dental health especially when taken on a
long-term basis. Evidence to support this concern was
provided by a study conducted in 1979 by Roberts and Roberts
[1], in which the dental health of a number of chronically
sick children taking oral medication long-term was compared
to that of a control group in which long term medication was
taken in a solid dosage form or the child was on no
medication. In their study, the researchers looked at the
dental health of 44 children aged under 6 years who had been
taking syrup medicines for at least 6 months. Results
showed that the children on long-term sugar-based medicines
had a mean score of decayed, missing, or filled deciduous
tooth surfaces (dmfs) of 5.6, which was significantly higher
than the dmfs score found in the control group of 47
children of similar age who were either on no medication or
medication in solid dose form (dmfs=1.3). That a certain,
already vulnerable group in the child population, namely,
those children who are in need of long-term medication for a
chronic disease should in addition become a group more
susceptible to dental disease through adherence to their
medication regime gives much cause for concern; the
treatment of dental disease in this group of children may be
more complicated, often necessitating the use of general
anaesthetics on an in-patient basis, and in consequence, the
dental treatment of these children is associated with a
higher morbidity than for a normal group of children. In
the overall assessment of the size of the problem of the
chronic use of liquid oral medication, necessary in the
planning and targeting for preventive measures, one
difficulty has been to work out what proportion of the
population may be at risk from the long-term use of liquid
medication. Because of this, a study was started 2 years
ago, in the departments of Child Dental Health and Oral
Biology at Newcastle Dental School, to survey the use of
liquid oral medication in children in a number of districts
in the Northern Region.

AIMS OF THE STUDY

Main Aim

1) To determine the prevalence of frequent administration of liquid oral medication long-term in children aged 1-16 years in a number of districts within the Northern Region. For the purposes of the study, 'frequent' was taken to be daily use, and 'long-term', for 3 months or longer. The districts involved were Newcastle, Gateshead, North and South Tyneside and Northumberland.

Subsidiary Aims

1) To determine the medical problems for which liquid oral medicines are used long-term.
2) To determine the age and sex profile of those children taking long-term liquid oral medication.
3) To determine the sweetening agents used in liquid oral medicines for long-term use.
In addition, two other aspects of the study determined;
4) The volume of liquid oral medication consumed within the Northern Region during a one year period.
5) For Great Britain, the Northern Region and some Family Practitioner Committees (Newcastle, North and South Tyneside) the number of prescriptions and volume of liquid medicines prescribed during a one year period.

OVERVIEW OF PRESCRIBING AND DISPENSING OF MEDICINES IN THE U.K.

The nature of prescribing and dispensing of prescriptions for long-term use, together with the massive consumption of Over- The-Counter (OTC) products, both long and short-term, in this country necessitates that a survey of use should consider all the means by which liquid medicines are procured and consumed.

Figure 1. Routes for prescribing and dispensing of medicines in the U.K. (sources of information).

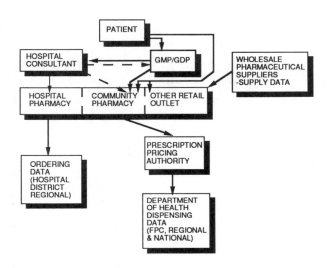

Figure 1 indicates the way in which medicines are prescribed by hospital and general practitioner services in this country.

In normal circumstances, for a medical problem of minor significance such as a cough or cold, a local pharmacy would usually be approached for advice and an over-the-counter (OTC) product such as an analgesic or cough linctus purchased for self administration. For those attending their own doctor, [General Medical Practitioner (GMP)], once the problem was diagnosed, the GMP may provide a prescription which is then taken to a local pharmacist for dispensing.

However, for a recurring or complex problem, the GMP may feel that referral for a consultant opinion is necessary. Upon referral, the hospital consultant will see the patient, diagnose the problem and, if medication is required, will supply the first prescription on the hospital prescription form [FP14(HP)] which is dispensed in the hospital pharmacy in most instances. In a few instances, the prescription from the hospital doctor may be dispensed from the local pharmacy but this practise is more expensive for the health authority concerned and is therefore discouraged. The consultant will decide upon an appropriate interval to review the patient, will communicate his findings to the GMP and, if medication is involved, the GMP will be responsible for its provision, usually on a monthly basis under the guidance of the hospital physician. These medicines provided on prescription by GMPs, hospital physicians, and General Dental Practitioners (GDPs) are usually Prescription Only Medicines (POMs), that is, available only on medical or dental prescription.

Medicines bought Over-The-Counter are classified as Pharmacist only (P) drugs, dispensed only when the Pharmacist is on the premises, and General Sales List (GSL) medicines which can be bought through pharmacies or other retail outlets such as supermarkets. In a pharmacy, all prescriptions from GMPs and GDPs and a small number of hospital prescriptions arising from hospital out-patient clinics are processed by the pharmacist who is contracted by the Family Practitioner Committee to work within the National Health Service. The prescriptions are, each month, sorted by the name of the GMP or GDP and sent to the Prescription Pricing Authority (PPA), which is based in Newcastle Upon Tyne, for processing. The processing enables payment to be made to pharmacists, and a compilation of prescribing figures to be sent to each General Medical Practitioner to keep him informed of his prescribing patterns and costs on a monthly basis.

As far as obtaining information regarding consumption of liquid oral medicines, there are 3 main sources:- the Statistics and Research Division of the Department of Health compile dispensing figures from the PPA for prescribing of drugs, on a local Family Practitioner Committee basis, regionally and nationally. This is for all drug preparations, whether they be tablet, injection, liquid or other surgical preparations prescribed and dispensed through the General Medical, Dental and Pharmacy Services within the National Health Service. Each preparation has a separate drug number and is classified into a group of medicines according to therapeutic classification.

As far as hospital pharmacy dispensing data are concerned, nothing is comprehensively collected regarding the dispensing of medicines, but ordering data are compiled on a hospital, district and regional basis for all drug preparations ordered into hospital pharmacies.

Another source of information is the wholesale pharmaceutical suppliers. There are 4 main companies in the Northern Region supplying pharmacies within the whole range of POM, P only and GSL medicines.

METHODS

Overall, the study consisted of 5 aspects;
1) The Consultant Survey.
2) The General Medical Practice Survey.
3) A Prescription Analysis Survey.
4) A Hospital Pharmacy Ordering Survey.
5) A Wholesale Pharmaceutical Supply Survey.

The Consultant Survey and the General Medical Practice Survey were concerned with long-term medication in children and the rest with overall liquid oral medication consumption both long and short-term and for all ages. For the purposes of this paper only the two surveys primarily concerned with long-term medication, namely the Consultant Survey and the General Medical Practice Survey will be discussed further.

CONSULTANT SURVEY

Method

As far as the Consultant Survey was concerned, 5 districts

were selected to make the most efficient use of the manpower
available.

The Northern Region as a whole employs 65 Consultant
Paediatricians and contains a population of approximately
600,000 one to sixteen year-old children, which represents
approximately 19% of the total population of the Northern
Region which is 3.1 million.

The 5 districts selected employ 25 Consultant
Paediatricians, therefore approximately 1/3 of the
Consultant Paediatricians were involved within the 5
districts studied out of the 16 districts within the
Northern Region.

Once the protocol for the study had been agreed by all
the relevant Ethics Committees, the Consultant
Paediatricians employed in these districts were contacted
and an appointment made to visit them and discuss whether
they may have any children under their care who fulfilled
the study criteria. These were that the child should be
aged between one and sixteen years of age at the time of the
study, currently be taking a liquid oral preparation on a
daily or alternate day basis, and the medication would be of
long-standing duration i.e. three months or longer. A
proforma to record medication details was distributed for
completion. Population information to enable a calculation
of prevalence was obtained from the Tyne and Wear County
Wide Research and Intelligence unit and the Office of
Population Census and Surveys. As far as the identification
of the sweetener in a liquid oral medicine was concerned, a
number of sources of information were available. The
National Pharmaceutical Association publishes a listing of
sweetener content of liquid oral medicines for professional
use, mainly for the care of diabetics. Additionally, a
number of lists have appeared in the pharmaceutical
literature and these, together with the Data Sheet
Compendium compiled by the Association of the British
Pharmaceutical Industry (ABPI) and direct communication with
manufacturers, made the identification of the sweetening

agents in the liquid oral medicines possible.

Results and Discussion

Twenty two consultants, 3 senior registrars and 1 specialist in child health, had 190 children aged 1-16 years under their care who were taking liquid oral medication frequently for longer than 3 months.

Calculation of the prevalence of this practice is shown in table 1.

TABLE 1
Mid 1988 population estimate for all districts in the study and the prevalence of long-term liquid oral medication in 1-16 year olds.

	All ages	1-16 yr olds	%
Total (5 districts)	1,135,800	213,000	19%
Prevalence		190/213,000 = 0.09%	
1:1100 children aged 1-16 yrs of age in the 5 districts studied			

One hundred and ninety out of the population of 1-16 year olds in the districts studied represents a prevalence of 0.09%, that is, 1 in 1100 children between the ages of 1 and 16 years in the 5 districts studied were taking long-term liquid oral medication on a daily basis.

Analysis of the age distribution of these children indicates that a wide age range of children were taking medication in liquid oral form - 40% were below the age of 5, 43% aged 5-11, and 17% aged 12-16 (Table 2).

TABLE 2
The age distribution of the 190 children
(aged 1-16 years) taking liquid oral medication
for 3 months or longer at the time of the study.

Age(yrs)	No.	%
1-4	76	40%
5-11	82	43%
12-16	32	17%
Total	190	100%

Consideration of the 5 most prescribed liquids shows
that they fell into 3 groups of medicines - anticonvulsants,
laxatives and purgatives, and the group 'other anti-
infectives'. This group included such drugs as
cotrimoxazole and trimethoprim commonly used in recurrent
chest and urinary tract infections.

The actual medicines, in descending order of use, were
sodium valproate (41 patients), carbamazepine (25 patients)
and sennosides (17 patients) as shown in table 3.

TABLE 3
The five most prescribed liquid medicines
according to therapeutic classification.

Therapeutic classification	Liquid oral medicine	No. pre-scribed generi-cally	No. pre-scribed by propriet-ary name	No. of patients
014 Anticonvulsants	Sodium valproate	12	29	41
035 Laxatives & purgatives	Lactulose	28	1	29
089 Other anti-infectives	Cotrimoxazole	11	14	25
014 Anticonvulsants	Carbamazepine	7	18	25
035 Laxatives & purgatives	Sennosides	-	17	17
	Total	58	79	137

As far as the duration of the medication was concerned, for the 311 medicines taken by 190 children, 34% had been taken for between 3 and 12 months at the time of the study, 24% for 1-2 years and 31% for 2 years or more.

TABLE 4
The duration of long-term liquid oral medication
in the six most commonly prescribed therapeutic classes.

| Therapeutic class | Duration of medication | | | | |
	3-12 mo	1-2 yrs	2+ yrs	Unspec.	Total (base)
014 Anticonvulsants	13%	21%	56%	10%	100% (70)
035 Laxatives & purgatives	30%	21%	26%	23%	100% (47)
089 Other anti-infectives	26%	41%	28%	5%	100% (39)
121 Vitamin preparations	34%	31%	22%	13%	100% (32)
031 Antacids	28%	40%	20%	12%	100% (25)
052 Anti-asthmatics	64%	13%	9%	14%	100% (22)
Others	45%	17%	25%	13%	100% (76)
					(311)

Table 4 indicates the duration of medication at the time of the study according to the class of medicine for the six most commonly prescribed therapeutic classes in the study. The majority of anticonvulsant liquids had been taken for 2 or more years. For laxatives and purgatives, the duration of medication was evenly distributed, with similar proportions of children taking medication for each time period. The most popular time period for use of other anti-infectives such as cotrimoxazole and trimethoprim was 1-2 years, with 41% of these medicines used for this period,

26% used for 3-12 months and 28% for 2 or more years at the time of the study. The vitamin preparations tended to be used over a shorter period, with two-thirds of the 32 medicines involved being prescribed for up to 2 years. Forty percent of the antacid liquids were prescribed for 1-2 years and 64% of the anti-asthmatic liquids for 3-12 months. With the advent of the new generation of aerosols and nebulisers in the treatment of asthma, children as young as 2-2.5 years can now effectively use these alternatives to liquid oral medicines, reducing the time period for which liquid oral dose forms will be used in many cases.

Of the 190 children, the majority had epilepsy as the principal medical problem for which they were taking liquid oral medication. Fourteen percent were in chronic renal failure and taking a range of liquids. Eleven percent had constipation as their major medical problem and 9% were suffering from asthma requiring long-term liquid medication. Recurrent urinary tract infections were the fifth most common problem requiring the use of long-term liquid oral medication.

The sweetening agents contained in the 58 different liquid oral preparations taken by the 190 children is given in table 5.

TABLE 5
The sweetening agents contained in the
58 liquid oral medications used long-term.

	No.	%
Sugar	19	33%
Non-sugar	18	31%
Variable	21	36%
Total	58	100%

Thirty-three percent were sugar based, 31% non-sugar based and 36% were variable. The term 'variable' was used to describe liquids in which the sweetening agent could not be elucidated fully from the information given in the completed questionnaire.

Of the 19 sugar-containing medicines, 11 were sucrose-based, 3 contained Syrup BP, that is, 66.7% w/v of sucrose in solution. Various other combinations of sucrose and sorbitol, sucrose and ethanol, sucrose and saccharin, sucrose and liquid glucose, and lactose and galactose were used in the other 5 sugar-containing liquids.

Of the 10 sugar-free liquids, five contained saccharin and five sorbitol as the sole sweetening agent, and three had no sweetening agent at all (these three included the anti-convulsant drug phenobarbitone and the anti-psychotic agent haloperidol). Two sugar-free liquids contained sorbitol and saccharin, and saccharin and glycerol. Lycasin by itself and in combination with saccharin accounted for another 3 liquids.

If the sweetening agents used in the 5 most commonly prescribed long-term liquid oral medicines are considered more closely, sodium valproate was the most commonly prescribed medicine (in 41 instances). It is formulated as a sugar-based syrup containing sucrose, sorbitol and saccharin, and as a sorbitol and saccharin based liquid. The information regarding whether the liquid or syrup form of sodium valproate was being used by a child could not always be fully elucidated in the survey, and in many instances this was because the distinction was not made in the child's medical records. Both liquid and syrup are equivalent in terms of bio-availability but the liquid only came onto the market in 1983 whereas the syrup has been available since 1976. A reluctance of both patient and medical practitioner to change from a syrup form has presumably led to the persistence of the   manufacturers to continue to provide both formulations, and prescription analysis has shown wide use of the sugar-containing syrup with more than twice the number of prescriptions (149,700) for sodium valproate syrup dispensed in Great Britain in

1987 compared to the liquid version (22,900 prescriptions).

Lactulose is an open formula medicine; it can be made by any company under licence as long as it conforms to the standards laid down in the British Pharmacopeia. It contains a combination of lactose and galactose together with lactulose which is the active ingredient.

Carbamazepine, an anti-convulsant agent, is available in liquid form, non-sugar based only, and contains sorbitol and saccharin as sweetening agents.

Cotrimoxazole is another open formula medicine and available in 5 proprietary paediatric liquid formulations, two of which are non-sugar based, and at least 8 generic liquid preparations, all of which are sugar-based. All these preparations conform to the standards for cotrimoxazole BP. This is where the concept of variability becomes important; since there are no sugar-free generics, the only way a child can get a sugar-free product is if the prescriber specifies SF on the prescription, or if the prescription specifies a proprietary product which is sugar-free. This latter practice of prescribing by proprietary name is discouraged within the National Health Service by government anxious to cut its drugs bill.

Conclusions

One hundred and ninety children aged 1-16 years were identified as currently taking long-term liquid oral medicines (LOMs) frequently, under the care of consultant paediatricians. This represented a prevalence of 1 in 1100 or 0.09% of children in the 5 districts studied. Of the 190 children (112 male, 78 female) 40% were below the age of 5, and 43% aged 5-11 years. Fifty five percent had been taking LOMs for more than 1 year and 31% for more than 2 years. Of the 58 different liquid oral preparations taken long-term, 19 were sugars-containing and 18 sugars-free.

GENERAL MEDICAL PRACTICE SURVEY

Once the Consultant Survey was under way it became clear
that a number of children taking long-term medication would
never see a paediatrician and therefore would not be
included in the net cast for the consultant survey. In
addition, the fact that the interval between recalls for
some children is quite long would reduce the numbers
identified through the consultant survey. Therefore, it was
important to assess the extent of long-term medication use
in general medical practice, alongside the consultant
survey. The consultant caring for the child taking long-term
medication will refer the child back to the GMP from whence
he came once the problem was diagnosed. The month to month
prescribing of medicines is the responsibility of the GMP
usually under the guidance of the consultant who will review
the child at appropriate intervals which may be yearly or
longer. Children were most easily identified at recall
rather than from a list of patients except in 'on-call'
situations where the child may have to be ready for
treatment at short notice and, therefore, easily contacted.
It was decided that a survey of 4 General Medical Practices,
two in Northumberland and two in Newcastle should be
undertaken. In selecting from practices with comprehensive
computing facilities there would be a small bias in the
results, since practices which had computerised their
records were more likely to have introduced other
streamlining and efficiency practices, but this was
accepted.

With the help of the Family Practitioner Committees and
the Computer Facilitator for Northumberland, 4 practices
were chosen, each of which had a multiple partnership with a
large practice population of more than 5000 with a broad
age, sex and socio-economic range of patients. Ethics
Committee approval was gained for the project, the senior
partner in each practice contacted by letter and an
appointment arranged with them at which the study was
discussed, and practice details and information regarding

any patients on liquid oral medication long-term requested.

Results

The 4 practices included in the survey ranged in size between approximately 5000 and 14500 patients of all ages with a 1-16 year-old population of between 17% and 24% (Table 6).

TABLE 6
Details for the four General Medical Practices regarding
repeat prescribing and long term medication

	PRACTICE			
District	1 Newcastle	2 Newcastle	3 N'land.	4 N'land.
Total practice size (patients)	8632	5877	5050	14414
Total 1-16 yr. olds	1529	974	1187	2934
% 1-16 yr.olds	18%	17%	24%	20%
No. of repeat prescriptions/ month (all ages)	2500	1062	figure not available	960
No. of repeat prescriptions (1-16 yrs.) > 3 months (% of 1-16 yr. olds)	8(0.52%)	1(0.1%)	0(0%)	2(0.07%)
No. on long term LOMs & consultant paed. care (% of 1-16 yr. olds)	4(0.26%)	1(0.1%)	0(0%)	2(0.07%)

The number of repeat prescriptions handled each month varied by up to 2.5 times with one practice in Newcastle handling 2500/month and the large practice in Northumberland approximately 1000. There were between 0 and 8 repeat prescriptions for liquids for 1-16 year-olds distributed by the practices each month. Those children who were under the care of a consultant and taking LOMs repeatedly, varied from 50% to 100% of all those on repeat prescriptions, with a prevalence of between 0 and 0.52% of 1-16 year olds. Of the 11 children identified as taking repeat prescriptions of liquid oral medicines, five had epilepsy as their main medical problem, two of these were taking sodium valproate syrup, two were taking the liquid form of sodium valproate, one was on carbamazepine and one on the liquid sedative trimeprazine. Three of these five medicines were sugar-free.

The duration of medication ranged from 2-5 years and 4 out of the 5 children on anti-convulsant therapy were under consultant care. Of the other six children, three were asthmatics and had taken salbutamol liquid for up to 3 years at the time of the study, and two of these children were under the care of a consultant paediatrician.

Discussion

Overall, the results from the General Medical Practice were useful in that they showed that not all children taking long term medication are under hospital care. Of the 11 children identified in GMP practice as taking daily long-term medication for more than 3 months, 7 were under the care of consultants (Table 7).

TABLE 7
The prevalence of long-term liquid oral medication
in 1-16 year olds in the Northern Region

	GMP Survey (4 practices)	Consultant Survey (5 districts)
Population (1-16 yr olds)	6624	213,000
Total No. of children with long-term LOMs (consultant care)	7	190
Total No. of children with long-term LOMs (GMP & consultant care)	11	-
Prevalence (consultant care)	0.11%(1:900)	0.09%(1:1100)
Prevalence (GMP & consultant care)	0.17%(1:600)	-

EXTRAPOLATION:
Population (1-16 yr olds) Northern Region = 630,000

0.17% of 630,000 = approx. 1070 children could be expected to
be taking long-term LOMs in the Northern Region.

This indicated a prevalence of 0.11% or 1:900 children,
fairly similar to the consultant survey of 0.09% or 1:1100
children. However, there were a number of children who might
never see a consultant and take long-term liquids under the
care of GMPs only, therefore, the overall prevalence could be
0.17% or 1:600 children. If these figures are extrapolated,
0.17% of 630,000, (the population of 1-16 year olds in the
Northern Region) i.e. 1070 children, could be expected to be
taking long-term LOMs in the Northern Region.

Epilepsy was the main medical problem in General Medical
Practice for which long-term LOMs were taken. The children
with epilepsy were on liquid oral medication for extended
periods of more than six years in some cases. There was not
the natural progression on to tablets that tends to occur in
children with other diseases. In a number of instances this
was due to associated brain damage and developmental
retardation in the child, making the administration
of dosage forms other than liquids impossible.

Of the twelve LOMs taken long-term in the General Medical
Practice Survey, seven were sugar-free and five sugar-
containing.

OVERALL CONCLUSIONS

In the population of 630,000 1-16 year olds in the Northern
Region, 1070 could be expected to be taking long-term liquid
oral medication; this represented 1:600 children.

TABLE 8
Number of prescriptions (x1000) and quantities
(litres x1000) for all liquid oral medicines
prescribed and dispensed through general
medical and dental services in 1987.

	Prescriptions (x 1000)	Quantity (Litres x 1000)
Great Britain	43900	10323
Northern Region	2680	680

In addition to this, the large-scale use of over-the-
counter (OTC) liquid products (Table 8), many of which are
taken on a very regular basis (e.g. cough medicines and
analgesics) and many of which are sugar-based, means that a
significant proportion of the child population is subjected
to an increased sugar intake. Parents administering these
medicines may not be aware of this source of sugar and
unaware that their child is in greater danger of dental
disease because of this. Comprehensive dental preventive
measures should be available for these chronically sick
children as an adjunct to medical management, when there is
no alternative to sugar-based medicines for treatment of
their chronic illness.

Since the majority of prescriptions for long-term LOM use
in children are provided by General Medical Practitioners,
with or without the advice of hospital physicians,
information and support regarding the use of sugar-free

alternatives should be more forthcoming from the medical, dental and pharmacy professions.

Allied with the encouragement of doctors and dentists to prescribe generically, the Department of Health should tighten guidelines for the manufacture of generic medicines to encourage the provision of a suitable range of sugar-free liquid generic medicines likely to be used long-term.

ACKNOWLEDGEMENTS

The help and co-operation of the consultant physicians involved in the study, together with that of the Statistical Research Division of the Department of Health is gratefully acknowleged.

REFERENCES

1.   Roberts, I.F. and Roberts, G.J., (1979). Relation
        between medicines sweetened with sucrose and dental
        disease.
        Brit. Med. J. 1979, 2, 14-16.

FORMULATING SUGAR-FREE ORAL LIQUID
MEDICINES

S W BOND AND C D FIELDS
Consumer Healthcare Product Development
The Wellcome Foundation Ltd, Temple Hill,
Dartford, Kent DA13 ORY

ABSTRACT

Increased awareness of the possible detrimental effects on health of
excessive sucrose intake has produced a demand from both the consumer and
some governmental regulatory agencies for sugar-free oral liquid
medicines. The need for such formulations is particularly great in
children undergoing chronic medication with oral liquids. Over the past
decade the formulation of such liquid medicines has been facilitated by
the increased availability of suitable alternatives to sucrose. A number
of key factors are likely to influence the rate at which sugar-free
products reach the market place, the most important of which may be the
cost of these sucrose replacements and their general regulatory
acceptability.

INTRODUCTION

It was among the Arabs over a thousand years ago that cane sugar was first
utilised to impart palatability to medicines. The practice spread
eventually to Europe and was well established with English apothecaries by
the middle of the sixteenth century. However, in the recent past - over
the last decade or so - the adverse effects of sucrose ingestion in terms
of dental health and obesity (and its consequences) have become recognised
in the developed world causing indirectly pharmaceutical companies to
formulate sugar-free medicines.

For pharmaceutical companies attempting to formulate products to meet
international requirements, a number of factors influence the choice of
sucrose replacement. Essentially, these factors can be categorised into
commercial, medical, regulatory, manufacturing and formulatory although
all could be construed, in one way or another, as having an ultimate
commercial impact.

COMMERCIAL FACTORS

Prescription Products

Given the serious nature of the disease states they are designed to treat, it would seem a reasonable contention that oral liquid medicines available on prescription should not contribute in any way to the detriment of the health of the patient. However, many drugs are relatively unpalatable and this is likely to be exacerbated when they are presented in the form of an oral liquid. Unsurprisingly, therefore, large amounts of sucrose have been used in countless formulations to improve palatability and, by inference, patient compliance. It has not been uncommon for such products to contain in excess of 50% sucrose.

Generally, the target patient population for this type of medication is children and it is now well accepted that chronic therapy regimens of liquid medicines high in sucrose content can have a deleterious effect on dental health due to the high cariogenic potential of the medication. There is no doubt that this is the principal reason behind the issue of guidelines in a number of countries from governmental agencies dealing with the registration of medical products indicating that every effort should be made to formulate such oral liquid medicines without sucrose and other reducing sugars.

To date the most popular replacement for sucrose as a bulk sweetener seems to have been sorbitol. However, being a polyhydric alcohol of low gastro-intestinal absorption it tends to exert a considerable osmotic laxative effect in most individuals and a number of reports have indicated a reduced tolerance to this effect in severely incapacitated patients where medication is administered by nasogastric tube. Laxation and flatulence are common side effects with a number of bulk sweetening agents and the severity of effect in certain individuals needs to be balanced against the advantages the inclusion of such materials confer on any formulation.

Over-The-Counter Products

Despite significant health education activities, use and attitude surveys among consumers generally reveal limited enthusiasm for the sucrose-free medicine option. Although there does seem to be a geographical division of opinion within European countries, the basis for response seems to be on an emotional level because of the paediatric orientation of the products. In the north, enthusiasm is much stronger and tends to be associated with the move against potentially injurious additives such as dyes and preservatives. In the south, palatability remains the overriding factor despite the perceived health advantages that sucrose-free medicines could offer.

In the USA, few existing over-the-counter medicines contain anything other than sucrose as the bulk sweetening agent. Again, the market is oriented towards the paediatric sector and taste seems to be of overwhelming importance.

Although the introduction of sugar-free medicines may have had little to do with anything other than attempts to gain a commercial advantage in an increasingly competitive market, the resultant increase in availability of such products has had the benefit of offering increased choice to the consumer.

Material Costs

One of the major contributory factors influencing the move towards alternative bulk sweetening agents has been their relative cost in comparison to sucrose. An indication of relative costs is given in Table One.

The situation in Europe is exacerbated in that manufacturers can claim EEC export subsidies and production refunds on finished medicinal products containing sucrose. At present levels, this serves to diminish the price of sucrose by 30-40% and thereby increase the relative cost of the bulk sweeteners. The overall effect is to make the inclusion of bulk sweeteners other than sucrose a less financially attractive option unless the consumer is prepared to bear the increase in the cost of the finished product.

TABLE ONE
Relative cost of Bulk Sweetening Agents
in comparison with Sucrose

Bulk Liquid Sweetener	Approximate Increase in cost relative to Sucrose
Sorbitol 70% Solution	1
Sorbitol Powder	1.5
Lycasin 80/55	1.6
Maltitol	1.7
Isomalt	4
Mannitol	7
Xylitol	8

International Implications

The most obvious implication for a pharmaceutical manufacturer attempting to formulate sucrose-free products for international market is the difference in regulatory status that the various sweeteners have in these markets.

Hydrogenated glucose syrup has been used in liquid medicines in Europe for some years now but its regulatory acceptability in the USA, the major pharmaceutical market of the World, remains at an early stage in the approval process. Much the same is acesulfame K which in the USA is not yet permitted in liquid products, being limited to dry formulations presently.

Many of the new excipients have a limited source thereby necessitating transportation across the globe to various manufacturing sites of the pharmaceutical producer. In the case of bulk liquids transportation costs may be significant and the effect of the stability of the material during transportation needs to be well established if it is not to engender problems for the stability of the finished product.

In the developing world, governmental restrictions often prevent the importation of many excipients. The restrictions may take the form of high import tariffs, legislation that necessitates the use of locally available excipients and, in some cases, total local manufacture using locally sourced materials. While the health considerations may be somewhat different in these countries compared to the developed Western economies, the result for the international pharmaceutical manufacturer is a proliferation of alternative formulations each of which requires considerable resource to develop to the requisite standards of stability, efficacy and safety.

MANUFACTURING CONSIDERATIONS

The manufacturing implications of utilising alternative sweetening agents, particularly bulk sweeteners, would appear to be dependent upon the size of operation involved. In small scale manufacture, the impact of any such change is unlikely to be significant. However, for major producers of liquid medicines changes of this type could have far reaching consequences depending upon the existing methods of manufacture and the choice of bulk sweetener as the sucrose replacement.

Solid Bulk Sweeteners

The replacement of granulated sucrose with solid bulk sweeteners such as xylitol, sorbitol, mannitol etc is unlikely to cause major changes in manufacturing methodology and associated ancillary operations. Cost of transportation and problems of bulk storage should be little different than for sucrose. In certain territories where locally sourced sugar may be of poor quality its replacement with an imported alternative such as sorbitol powder may confer improved stability on the finished product thereby enhancing its commercial utility and thus minimising the impact of increased raw material cost.

Because of the excellent aqueous solubility of sucrose there is, in certain cases, some potential for an increase in processing time with replacement materials. Where the resultant solution is more viscous than a comparable sucrose-based product, the need for the provision of adequate equipment (pumps, mixers etc) to handle the material will require consideration. Clearly, equipment changes/modifications to process the non-sucrose alternatives will need to take into account the inherent capacities of the existing facilities.

Liquid Bulk Sweeteners

Many large manufacturers of oral liquid pharmaceuticals prefer to utilise liquid sucrose rather than granulated sucrose in order to reduce processing time by obviating the need to make up the syrup base *in situ*. This allows for greater output of product from the manufacturing facility. The consequence of such an approach is the need for the bulk storage of the liquid sucrose in order to meet the manufacturing demands.

Any move away from sucrose in this situation would be likely to have considerable ramifications. To begin with, it is unlikely that sucrose replacement in all formulations would be either universal or synchronous. Thus the spectre of the need for additional storage facilities would become apparent immediately. A choice would then have to be taken between the installation of dedicated storage facilities for each bulk sweetener, with the consequent proliferation of storage tanks, and multipurpose storage facilities.

In either event a number of necessary modifications to standard storage facilities for liquid sucrose would be required in order to handle the alternative bulk sweetener with efficiency. Forced air ventilation is needed to prevent microbial spoilage of the material at the air/liquid interface. Where the material is significantly more viscous than liquid sucrose over the normal range of environmental temperatures, the inclusion of a heating facility within the tanks would be prudent to aid handling and minimise transference times during processing and avoid crystallisation.

In circumstances where manufacturing demand for oral liquid products is low and the offtake of bulk sweeteners equally diminished, the likelihood is that the latter materials would be stored in drums or semi-bulk containers. In such a situation where the material itself is of significantly high viscosity, transference to the manufacturing vessel may be both difficult and time - consuming. Inevitably this will have a negative impact on processing times and, possibly, manufacturing costs.

FORMULATION STUDIES

The main aim in the formulation of any oral liquid medicine is the production of stable and palatable entity that is both safe and efficaceous.

Where sucrose is to be replaced by either intense sweeteners or bulk sweeteners or, indeed, a combination of both types, adequate characterisation of the drug(s) to be masked is a necessary first step. Once the scale of the formulation problem has been established, work can be undertaken to resolve the situation. In cases, where the drug imparts little or no taste, the choice of sweetener should be relatively simple and may be selected with regard to cost and consumer preference in taste terms. However, in many cases, the overriding taste is powerful and unpleasant. In these circumstances, the sweetening power of the agents under consideration needs to be taken into account. Table Two illustrates the relative sweetness of the most commonly used sweeteners relative to sucrose.

A number of over-the-counter products are deemed suitable for the medication of a wide age range. In such cases, and where appropriate, awareness of the acceptable daily intake of sweeteners is needed and the amount utilised tailored to both formulatory requirements and age/weight related intake limitations.

Product Stability

Intense sweeteners are, for the most part, either ionic or polar compounds which accounts for their high aqueous solubility. However, due to this inherent property they can engender serious stability problems in disperse formulations such as emulsions and suspensions because of their potential to interact with the polymer suspension systems. At its most minor, the interaction may initiate changes in the rheological behaviour of the system which, in the longer term, could adversely effect the shelf life of the product. More seriously, it may lead to the irreversible flocculation of the dispersed particles rendering it unacceptable in terms of dose homogeneity in addition to physical stability. Although manipulation of the processing method may limit the effects of such interactions, less than robust formulations must be considered a liability given the extent of resource they require to support them during production scale manufacture.

TABLE TWO

Relative sweetness of commonly used sweeteners relative to sucrose

Sweeteners	Relative Sweetness to Sucrose
Sorbitol	0.5
Isomalt	0.5
Hydrogenated Glucose Syrup	0.75
Maltitol	0.9
Xylitol	1
Cyclamate and Salts	30
Acesulfame K	200
Aspartame	200
Saccharin and Salts	300
Thaumatin	2000

The interactions of the intense sweeteners within disperse formulations may also manifest itself with time as a reduced taste-masking capacity. More well-known, perhaps, is the tendency for aspartame to hydrolyse in aqueous media thus minimising its potential for inclusion in oral liquid pharmaceutical formulations which demand no significant change in stability profile for periods of two years and above.

In formulations of disperse systems, the hydrophillic nature of the bulk sweeteners such as sorbitol and hydrogenated glucose syrup may reduce the extent of hydration of the polymeric cellulose materials utilised as suspending agents. The consequence of this is a potential for changes in rheological profile of a product over its shelf life which, in certain cases, could have a negative effect on the physical stability.

The high affinity of polyols for water can also have a deleterious effect on the inherent solvent capacity of a formulation. This may lead to solubility problems with active ingredients and preservatives which in turn may have an adverse influence on dose homogeneity and preservative efficacy.

The replacement of sucrose with other sweetening agents may also contribute much to the enhancement of the stability of certain drug substances in solution. It is known that reducing sugars and their acid residues, which may be either present or have the potential to be formed in sucrose-based medicines, can have an adverse effect on the chemical stability of certain drugs. Replacement with materials such as sorbitol, hydrogenated glucose syrup etc may have a significant effect in improving the shelf life of formulations containing susceptible active ingredients.

CONCLUSIONS

There can be little doubt that the replacement of sucrose in medicines will make some contribution to overall improvements in health when associated with a general reduction in dietary sucrose intake. However, it would be unwise to overlook some of the potential adverse effects of the replacement materials.

The principal factors militating against the more rapid replacement of sucrose in medicines are the slow and irregular approval of alternatives in the major markets, the increased costs associated with the purchase of these alternatives, the need for further product development activities and the requirement for the registration and approval of the formulated products.

PRESCRIBING SUGAR-FREE LIQUID ORAL MEDICINES

DR. GEORGE M. MITCHELL
University of Wales College of Medicine
Heath Park, Cardiff   CF4 4XN

ABSTRACT

The sucrose content of liquid medications is one factor which can be controlled. Preparations for children should not be diluted with syrup and pharmacists should be authorised to substitute sugar-free preparations for young and old. Dentists must influence the public regarding the dangers of sucrose on children's teeth. There must be persuasion of both the pharmaceutical manufacturers to supply sugar-free preparations and the Government to make available suitable measuring devices to be used for the accurate administration of liquid medication, without dilution, to children.

TEXT

For the last two days you have been discussing the disadvantages and difficulties associated with sucrose and the production of caries.

The desire for 'sweet tasting' medicines is universal. The phrase 'I hope it tastes nice' is commonplace. Sugar is not a new commodity. It has been grown in India since 3rd Century B.C. The stalk of the sugar cane is the most interesting part and even today, in the streets of India, you can see stalls fitted with rollers which squeeze the stalk and you drink the juice. Think of the caries in India - interestingly enough you see little caries in young children in hospital in India.

At the present moment we use over 90 million tons of sugar per annum and this is in addition to the various synthetic sweeteners. However, we must ask the question 'why did we use sucrose in the first place ?'

Probably for the following reasons:

. Prevents bacterial contamination
. Has antioxidant properties
. Is a bulking agent
. Cheap and easy to process
. Available in pure drug stable form

As a result, sucrose has been prescribed extensively over the years and it is the <u>single factor</u> which we can control in medicines and so help to reduce caries in children.

Sucrose is broken down by oral microorganisms and acidic products drop the pH value in dental plaque to the acidic side(1) in the following manner:

1. Carbohydrates are taken up by bacterial layer on the tooth.
2. Organisms ferment sugars and produce acid.
3. These acids in plaque attack enamel and this may produce a cavity.

The acid causes demineralisation of the enamel which may lead to cavitation. Of the three components, the excess carbohydrate is one with which we can easily deal.

So we can accept that the more frequently sugars are consumed the greater the risk of dental disease in erupted teeth. However, to the sucrose medicines, we must also add - the consumption of snacks between meals, the continued use of non-prescription pharmaceuticals, sweets, chocolates, chewing gums, drinks (and now choc-ice) all of which contain sugars. Many of these contain 15% - 20% sucrose.

Over-the-counter pharmaceutical mixtures and preparations have been a problem, since most of them contain sucrose. Some manufacturers are now removing the sucrose from these preparations. However, many still contain sucrose and those with 15% - 20% sucrose are potentially cariogenic and, if they contain a higher percentage of sugar, they are more cariogenic.

In a sample of 226 products, 155 contained sucrose. Over 90% of these contained more than 15% sucrose and 68% contained 40% to 90% sucrose. Thus, many such products are potent cariogenic agents(2).

When we prescribe for a child we must remember that a child is not just a small adult. Over the years we have paid lip service to this fact and calculated dosage based on body weight. This is empirical and has no scientific validation. We have given out prescriptions often with little justification. It is better to avoid all pharmacological agents except for serious illness when drugs may be necessary. In other words keep drugs for essential treatment. We do not require drug treatment at all times.

Chronically sick children or children with repeated bouts of acute illness are often required to take medicines on a long-term basis(3).

This now raises the question 'which preparations are available ?' These can be classed as follows:

- . Liquid preparations - simple solutions
- . Soluble preparations - tablets
- . Suspended preparations
- . Chewable
- . Capsules
- . Injections

From the prescriber's point of view, a simple liquid preparation is the easiest to give to the child, and a sweetened preparation improves the palatability and also the compliance of the patient - young or old.

In order to administer the mixture to a child, we usually use the 5 ml teaspoon for the dose. An alternative way of measuring quantities of liquid oral medicines is to use a syringe such as the one shown in the illustration. Sometimes the dose is contained in a smaller volume and then the pharmacist has to make the volume up to 5 ml and this is done using syrup.

We really should think of ways of giving liquid without sucrose to children. The British National Formulary (BNF) stresses the importance of excluding sugar from medicines for children and lists preparations which do not contain sucrose. There is also the possibility of using the rectal route which can be useful.

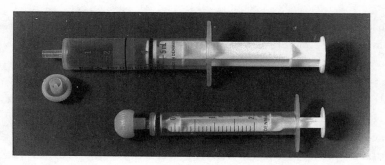

Illustration of syringe used for measuring liquid medicines

This then leads us to the question of how are we to arrive at a suitable sucrose-free liquid preparation ?

There are many sucrose substitutes on the market most of which are synthetic substances and we must remember that they may have toxic effects on our patients. The following are some of the alternatives.

Saccharin

Saccharin was first discovered in 1886 and came into prominence during two world wars. In the 1970's there was a study where rats were fed on a diet containing 5% saccharin. This study was followed for 2 generations and showed an increase in urinary bladder carcinoma in males compared with normal controls. There have been many human studies and, to date, only one Canadian and one Dutch study support the rat story. Saccharin may also cause skin defects, e.g. Urticaria.

Aspartame

Aspartame is about 180 times as sweet as sugar. It is a methyl-ester which is hydrolysed in the intestine to methanol, aspartic acid and phenylalanine. Methanol is produced but the amount circulating in blood is so small that it is unlikely to produce toxicity. Aspartic acid is similar to glutamate and may cause the so-called 'Chinese Restaurant Syndrome', i.e. pain in chest, flushing of face, numbness in face and neck. This is a risk for glutamate-sensitive persons. The most important effect is the raised phenylalanine in persons with phenylketonuria and this may lead to mental retardation. Also reported have been neurological effects, gastro-intestinal upsets and allergic type symptoms.

Cyclamate

Cyclamate is sodium cyclohexyl sulphamate and is fifty times sweeter than sucrose. In 1953 it was allowed to be used. But, in a two-year study, it produced urinary bladder carcinoma in rats and its use was stopped in 1970. In 1978, US courts upheld that it was unsafe, but in 1980 it was said to be safe and its use was limited to 800 mg/L.

Sorbitol

Sorbitol occurs in fruits and is half the sweetness of sucrose. It is a polyhydric alcohol. A 70% solution may be used. Since it is only slowly absorbed from the gut, water is retained due to osmotic pressure and diarrhoea may result. In some ways it is similar to glucose but it is not fermented by oral micro-organisms and has little acid-producing effect in plaque. It is considered to be non-cariogenic.

Xylitol is a five carbon alcohol and can be used in chewing gums.

Dihydrochalcones

Dihydrochalcones reduce bioflavinoids in citrus fruits. The compound most likely to be useful is Neohesperidin. Neohesperidin dihydrochloric (from seville oranges) is three hundred times sweeter than sucrose and can mask bitter tastes. It has no licence yet as safety tests have not yet been adequate enough.

Glycyrrhin

This is the sweet component of liquorice. The extract is used to sweeten tobaccos and as a flavouring agent and humectant. It is used in confections and chocolate, and is fifty times sweeter than sucrose. It could be used to sweeten dentifrices.

Adverse effects are not limited to the sweetening agents. Even the colouring substances we use for mixtures and tablets may have an effect. For example, tartrazine used to colour liquids and tablets yellow may precipitate asthmatic attacks.

DISCUSSION AND SUMMARY

The final question is "what are we to do" ? The following ten points should be considered:

(1) Education of the young and old regarding the dangers of sucrose.

(2) The pharmacist should act as a counsellor regarding sucrose-free mixtures and should urge people to seek dental advice.

(3) Formulations should be devised which are free of sucrose. This usually means a major reformulation and not just a simple substitution of another sweetener.

(4) Syrup must not be used as a diluent.

(5) All sugar-containing medicines should be labelled, with the concentration of sugar specified as g/ml.

(6) Medical Practitioners must be encouraged to prescribe sugar-free preparations where possible.

(7) Pharmacists should be allowed to dispense sugar-free preparations rather than those containing sugar.

(8) The sugar-containing medications should be given at meal-times rather than between meals.

(9) Young and old should be encouraged to brush their teeth after taking medication.

(10) The pharmaceutical manufacturers should be encouraged to replace sucrose in their formulations.

REFERENCES

1. Rugg-Gunn, A.J. and Edgar, W.M., Sugar and dental caries: a review of the evidence. Community Dental Health, 1984, **1**, 85-92.

2. Babington, M.A. and Spadaro, D.C., Cariogenic Medications. Paediatric Nursing, 1982, **8**, 165-171.

3. Hobson, P., Sugar based medicines and dental disease. Community Dental Health, 1985, **2**, 57-62.

4. Rugg-Gunn, A.J. and Edgar, W.M., Sweeteners and dental health. Community Dental Health, 1985, **2**, 213-223.

DENTAL HEALTH EDUCATION AND PROMOTION

FRANK LEDWITH
Department of Education, University of Manchester,
Oxford Road, Manchester 60.

ABSTRACT

Conventional health education is based on the premises that the major determinants of health lie in individual behaviour and that individuals indulge in health harming behaviours due to ignorance. Both premises can be shown to be false by a wealth of evidence which show that social circumstances are the main determiners of health. It is suggested that the promotion of dental health should be mainly based on groups of people rather than individuals and that there must be efforts to counter the enormous power and influence of the sugar and confectionery industries. There is a need for education of dental health promoters to ensure that they understand the politics of their task. With due caution it should be possible to collaborate with some commercial interests to promote dental health, whilst being wary of being compromised into ineffectiveness.

INTRODUCTION

My background is that of a social science teacher and researcher who wandered into the area of health education and promotion, particularly in the area of smoking prevention, both as a campaigner and evaluator of the work of others. I have also seen a good deal of the power of commercial anti-health forces aided by the neglect of health considerations by governments in the UK. Recently I carried out an overview evaluation of a dental health

education campaign in a Regional Health Authority, which
is the basis of any detailed knowledge I have of dental
health issues. I want to present a challenge to
conventional notions of health education and suggest what
we might do in the way of the promotion of dental health.
Most of the broad basis of analysis will be drawn from
epidemiological evidence of the major killer diseases
where there is the most detailed and credible evidence.

The intellectual basis of conventional health education
is that:
a) the basis of the ill health targeted lies in the
behaviour of individuals and
b) that the individuals practising the behaviours do so
out of ignorance.
The belief is that if people are informed of the risks,
they will change their behaviour and the ill health will
be reduced. There is a whole wealth of evidence to
suggest that both propositions are substantially untrue.
Thus I am not at all sure that the practice of health
education is an intellectually honest or ethical
activity. I have some sympathy with the views of one
recent speaker at the British Association who suggested
that health education shows a 'worthy dishonesty' in that
it is based on the premise that 'the broadcasting of
propaganda, based on half-truth, simplification and
distortion is a legitimate use of public funds, so long

as the goal of the enterprise is the good of the community.'[1] However I am not sure whether I would place the stress on the worthiness or the dishonesty.

THE DETERMINANTS OF HEALTH

I would like to provide a broad outline of the main determinants of the health of any individual. These are:

- country of residence,
- occupational class,
- age.

The evidence that these are key factors is given below.

Country

The expectation of life at birth for males varies greatly from one country to another, from under 50 in some third world countries to well over 70 in others.[2] Within the industrial countries there are still some considerable variations. Japan for example has a life expectancy life in men at age 65 of 15.9 years (and increasing rapidly), compared with 13.5 in Britain.[3] Level of industrialisation is not the only important variable. Cuba for example has a life expectancy at age 65 higher than any country but Japan.[4] Even within countries there may be sometimes large variations by social group: in some areas of New York the expectation of life in young black men is lower than that in Bangladesh.[5]

Occupational Class

Within industrial societies, the death rates are consistently higher in those working in unskilled occupations, by a factor of typically 2-3 to 1.[6] This effect is not directly a consequence of the conditions of employment since the same gradients are found in the wives and the children of men of different social classes. The differences in death rates are linked to levels of education, to income, to type of housing and whether employed or unemployed. Contrary to popular myth, heart disease affects labourers more than executives with their supposedly high stress jobs and high fat executive lunches.

Age

The impact of age on life expectancy is obvious: the older you are the shorter your expected span, though the steepness of the gradient will vary. As noted above Japan has remarkably good gradient.

Behavioural effects

Note that within the factors listed there has as yet been no mention of individual behaviour. Within industrialised societies the amount of tobacco and alcohol consumed, the levels of ingestion of saturated fats and of sugars and the amount of exercise are linked to longevity. Thus the first questions to be asked above occupational class. Had politicians from the present government been asking the questions these would certainly have been the first. Though politically convenient they would have been barking up the wrong tree. Marmot[7] has carried out a prospective detailed study of male civil servants which avoids many of the possible statistical artefacts which might distort measures across different individuals. He studied civil servants from messenger grades to senior executives, assessing their state of health and life style, following them up for 10 years. He found that the lowest grades had a 2.7:1 risk of death from Coronary Heart Disease compared with the highest grade when controlling for age. The messenger grades did smoke more, had higher blood pressure, more obesity, more diabetes, were shorter and had less leisure time activity. However even when all these risk factors were taken into account, the differences in risk ratio was still 2.1:1. In other words the behavioural and other known risk factors accounted for less than half the differences in mortality, a finding which accords with other longitudinal studies in the USA such as the Alameda County study.[8]

Health not illness

The research quoted so far has had to do with death as a measure of health. The reason for this is that these are the most widely available data on health. However if we look at the less tangible aspects of actual health, the key questions would still be the same, though I have to say the data are much less robust and detailed. There is some evidence on morbidity. [9] There are higher rates of depression, of long-standing illness, of lack of well being associated with lower socio-economic class and of increasing age. Such measures are typically seen as lacking the hardness and clarity of mortality data and thus are often dismissed by most medical scientists. However it should be remembered that a simple question on "How is your health" has been found to be a predictor of longevity, independent of any medical assessment of health and may even be better predictor than such medical assessment.[10]

Social factors in health

The authors of the Alameda county study referred to above concluded, on the basis of their own and related work that "studies investigating the association between socio-economic status and disease have suggested that differences in behavioral risk factors...do not account for much of the association' They found that the area of residence had a more powerful effect than individual behaviour on longevity.

One of the most remarkable tables of statistics I have ever seen was produced in Newcastle, and concerned the relationship between area of residence, social class and health. Table 1 shows these findings of Professor Townsend and colleagues [11] who examined the crude premature death rates (that is before age 65 years) per 1000 men in areas of high and low overall mortality within the Northern Regional Health Authority. The main findings of the study were that the great majority of the variance between areas in death rates could be accounted for by 4 variables which measured access to resources: the percentage of owner occupied houses, of families with cars, of unemployed and of over-crowded housing. However the study of individual areas is very instructive.

Table 1

Crude premature death rates for economically active men aged 16-64 by high and low mortality areas

Death Rates per 1000

Social Class	Worst areas	Best areas
I and II	5.0	2.5
IV and V	8.9	3.7

It is remarkable that the death rates for manual workers (Classes IV and V) in the best areas are lower than that for professional and managerial classes in the worst areas. Note too, a point I will return to later, that the gap between social groups was also lower in the better areas. Lest this seem an isolated phenomenon or only concerned with death, a study by Byrne and Harrisson[12]

on self reported symptoms and subjective states of health
in Gateshead public housing produced similar data. They
found that it was not so much the type of residence
(tower block, flat or house) as the area of residence
which determined peoples' health. What are
euphemistically called "hard to let areas" were in fact
"hard to live in areas".

Blaxter[13] has been able to add to this analysis by
examining individual behaviours and areas of residence in
relation to health. Although she found that working class
people were more likely to indulge in various health
harming practices there was no great clustering of health
related behaviours: there were few people who indulged in
all the risky behaviours of smoking, drinking
excessively, having a poor diet and taking little
exercise. Just as Pill and Roisin[14] had found, the myth
of the feckless working class was just that, a useful
myth for politicians (which it must be noted is accepted
by many guardians of the public health who should know
better). However she concluded that "Circumstances,
including social support have been shown to carry more
weight for health outcomes than behaviour....Risk factors
are certainly related to health ...however they are often
more closely associated in good social circumstances and
environments than in poor."
Thus the first plank of the conventional health educator

platform (that individual behaviour is the main determinant of health) is seen to be shaky if not positively worm eaten. The second (that people behave in health threatening ways from ignorance) can rapidly be demolished. Most people in this country can tell you what are the main determinants behavioural determinants of health. Most smokers know that smoking is dangerous. If you ask, as I have in surveys, what are the main risk factors, then people will tell you: smoking, drinking, high fat and low fibre diet, lack of exercise and stress. It is true that those who do indulge in unhealthy behaviours will have various self deluding justifications but who are we to criticise: the self delusions of health educators and public health doctors in accepting an individualistic explanations of ill health which are politically much more acceptable are no less reprehensible since they are paid to know better.

HEALTH EDUCATION AND THE OPPOSITION

Given the evidence I have presented, which I accept, why would I want to associate myself with health education? Why would I accept employment to evaluate a dental health education campaign? I think my reasons arise mainly from my attitude to the opposition, to those who seek to undermine positive messages for health.
There is a war going on out there, where the anti-health

forces, the tobacco and alcohol industries, much of the processed food industry, the armaments industry and other industries promoting unhealthy products such as motor cars will spend very large amounts of money to persuade people to buy products which are harmful if not lethal to themselves and/or destructive of the environment, which is our home and that of our children. In this war it is not possible to be neutral. If you are not active in the cause of health, then you are on the side of ill health and death. As Edmund Burke has said "For evil to triumph it is only necessary for good men to do nothing". Given the choice, and lacking yet any coherent third way which is properly funded to make much impact, then there is to me only one choice, to support the pro-health rather than anti-health forces.

I could wax indignantly lyrical with tales of the evil activities of the tobacco industry in ensuring that, as sales of cigarettes stagnate in industrialised countries, they concentrate their efforts in third world countries aided by the US State Department amongst others. However I will confine my detailed comments to the sugar industry, once having introduced the general topic of the determinants of dental health.

DENTAL HEALTH

The epidemiology of dental health is well documented within its own narrow frame of reference. Murray's book

on "The Prevention of Dental Disease"[15] summarises the
main evidence on the effects of diet, of dental hygiene,
of fluoride and of dental treatment. The chapter by John
Beal comes closest to the more general findings I have
outlined above when he adopts an approach based on
people, on their attitudes and on their social groupings.
Poorer dental health, less knowledge of the factors
affecting dental health, less use of dentists , more
frequent health damaging behaviour and less stress on
prevention are to be found in working class people. It is
noted too that they would have less money to pay for
treatments and are more likely not to be able to partake
of these during working hours without loss of pay. There
is a subtle put-down in suggesting that the core attitude
is for immediate gratification rather than a future
orientation of the middle classes which would take a
lengthy analysis to challenge properly. (For the present
suffice it to refer to Julian Le Grand's[16] purely
economic analysis where health is regarded as an
investment with costs of upkeep and benefits of
longevity. Where the costs are higher and the benefits
are likely to be lower, as they would be for working
class people, then the purely rational economic
calculation would be to invest less, to "eat, drink and
be merry, for tomorrow we die.") To put it another way,
if you have an old car which threatens to fall apart
fairly soon, you are unlikely to spend much money in

servicing it.

What I find particularly interesting in Beal's
presentation of social factors is that, from his own
work, he reports that "dental behaviour was much more
strongly related to area of residence than any of the
other social variables" (such as income, education, type
of housing and voting behaviour). I would expect that the
same would be found to be true for actual dental health,
and not because of any strong direct link between
behaviour and dental health. The direct evidence for this
assertion is slim, but I have no reason to doubt that
dental health will be as much affected by social and area
circumstances as much as are the likelihood of heart
disease, major cancers and poor mental health.

Dental health education
The comments about peoples' adequate knowledge of what
constitutes good practice appears to be largely true with
respect to dental health. As part of the Regional dental
health campaign mentioned earlier, in a survey of dental
health practices amongst working class mothers of under
5s in Manchester[17], over 90% could identify key factors
likely to cause tooth decay: eating sweet things through
the day, eating sugary foods and drinks at mealtimes, not
brushing teeth regularly or well enough and not going to
the dentist regularly. There were a few areas of poorer

knowledge, for example not realising the importance of frequency as opposed to amount of sugary food intake and that decay in first teeth is important for longer term dental health. The majority of women felt (quite correctly) that they were well informed on aspects of dental health. A bare majority claimed to take their children to the dentist regularly. If, as seems likely, they were a representative sample then the claim owed more to what the mothers knew they should do than what they actually did. And therein lies the problem: the women knew what they should do but, like the rest of us, they very often did not do it.

Nonetheless a remarkably successful (within its conceptual limits) health education campaign was launched in the North Western Region targeted at the mothers of under 5s to remind them of the facts they already knew and to seek to prod them into changing their behaviour towards not giving so many sweet foods to their offspring. Some striking posters were developed to be shown on billboards and street level sites. In addition workshops were given for health visitors on aspects of dental health, with encouragement to pass on the messages to mothers of young children during routine visits. Over 50% of the target group recognised the posters and a remarkable 9% could remember the message of one poster without prompting. Health visitors reported having gained much authoritative knowledge from the workshops and most reported that they were more likely to pass on the knowledge to mothers.[18]

There were as well other aspects of the campaign, notably a workplace based initiative providing information and advice and an inspection and treatment scheme for primary school children in areas of poor uptake of dental treatment.

Overall the health education activities were positive in their results in reminding people of what they knew already. An in-depth study of a small number of mothers suggested that they found the reminders useful. And yet it is still true that the problems were seen to be located within the individual. The mothers who said they were most strict in restricting sugar intake were those with babies. Those who were struggling just to survive, and those with older toddlers were more likely to give in to the childrens' demands for sweet foods. As toddlers grow up they begin to be more affected by the sweets oriented culture around them and to be more exposed and influenced by TV and other advertising which would directly contradict the wishes of anyone who cares for their childrens' dental health. It is likely that those who live in comfortable circumstances would say that the mothers should remain strict and would have little sympathy for young women living in poverty and inadequate housing. They would not understand the situation of families living for several years in one room in bed and breakfast accommodation with no cooking facilities or play areas for the children. Lest this seem to be concentrating on the rare cases, it should be remembered that one quarter of Britain's children live at or below the poverty level[19].

THE FOOD INDUSTRY

A recent survey has shown that over half the advertisements on one week's childrens' TV were for food and soft drinks, far higher than for any other category and the majority of these ads were for sugar cereals or confectionery.[20] Many of the goods were claimed to be 'wholesome' or 'bursting with goodness'. Exciting animations predominated and there was extensive use of children to sell to children, a technique which would be banned in many countries. The target audiences are often too young to know the difference between adverts and programmes and even amongst the older children who might appreciate the difference the effects were powerful: two classes of eight year-olds rated Tony the Tiger (from the Frosties ad) more favourably than their class teacher. Belgium, Denmark and Sweden ban all ads aimed at children whilst other insist on health warnings. It has been found that children as young as four spend 20 hours a week watching TV and working class children watch over twice as much TV as higher income families.

There is a code of practice regarding TV advertising promulgated by the Independent Broadcasting Authority which has to be regarded as an elaborate joke at the expense of the public. The code states that 'No product may be advertised... which large numbers of children are likely to see which might result in harm to them is acceptable for some or for not very large numbers of children to see adverts for products which might result in physical harm. A moment's reflection should be enough to allow the full perversity of that premise to sink in. In addition the code states that 'advertisements shall not encourage persistent sweet eating during the day'. Presumably just encouraging sweet eating is acceptable. The children themselves can be left to make the connection that if one sweet is a good thing then regular sweets are even better. A child of two could probably make the inference which appears to be beyond the Independent Broadcasting Authority.

Not that I am suggesting that the worthy people who drew up the code, no doubt in consultation with the sugar and advertising industries, are stupid. Rather that they have had to engage in a charade of proper regulation, knowing of the government's unwillingness to legislate to control the activities of private industry, no matter how damaging. They have therefore, as has happened in the case of codes governing advertising of cigarettes, to agree a code with the industry acting as equals in the negotiation process. The form of words agreed are likely therefore to be either strictly nonsensical or capable of so wide an interpretation as to be no restraint to an imaginative advertising agency. It is interesting that the sugar bureau is not as far in retreat in intellectual argument as is the tobacco industry. In the 1960s and 70s the tobacco industry would still try to carry the argument on scientific grounds that smoking was not proven as a cause of ill health. After that argument was lost by the weight of evidence the assertion shifted to suggest that there was no proof that advertising or sponsorship encouraged anyone to smoke but that in merely encouraged switching from one brand to another, an effect which has never been claimed by any but the tobacco and alcohol industry as far as I know and which, if true, would destroy the macro-economic case for any form of advertising.

I published some research which suggested that the promotion by the tobacco industry of sports on TV acted as advertising to children[21]. I was then approached by a professor of marketing, hired by the industry, who wanted to examine my methodology and data in detail. The industry rejected my conditions that I would share my data if the tobacco industry would share theirs with me. Subsequently I was asked by the Market Reseach Society if they could examine my data and methodology. I then asked whence had arisen the idea of such an audit and what other research had been so audited with what results. The outcome was that I heard no more.

The sugar industry seems still seems to challenge the scientific evidence, unlike the tobacco industry. There are still scientists and scientific establishments wheeled out to put forward the industry line. In another capacity I have occasional contact with BBC radio and TV producers who make programmes about health matters. There are several BBC programmes which have been made about sugar and health which have never been shown as a result of pressure from the sugar industry. One producer told me that, in his experience, the sugar industry was the most powerful of all in challenging and silencing any planned broadcast which challenged their views. The Health Education Authority has had to be very cautious in any advice it publishes about the pernicious effects of sugar. It is true that they, along with the BBC, have been subject to political pressures but the government itself is not immune: the recent report on sugar from the Committee on the Medical Aspects of Food (COMA) had its main positive conclusions on the harmful effects of extrinsic sugar muted by the way it was presented. The Department of Health Press Release and the statement of a health minister concentrated on those areas where the case against sugar had been said to be unproven and suggested overall that sugar had been concluded not to be harmful for health.

The Regional dental health campaign I described above provided several examples of the methods of the sugar industry. The Sugar Bureau, which represents the industry, tried to use its membership of the British Dental Health Foundation to use that august body to stop the publication of its very effective posters on the damage which sugar can cause to young baby's teeth. The Sugar Bureau's Deputy Director wrote to the Foundation, twice referring to the Bureau's membership and to its sponsorship of the Foundation's leaflet on "Balancing Your Diet". She urged the Foundation to write to the minister to protest about the campaign messages, though asking that the letter be treated in the "strictest confidence". The Foundation did then write to the HEA complaining that the strong messages might deter people from going to the dentist and sugar was only one cause of dental decay.[22] By circumstances I cannot disclose the Bureau's letter came into the hands of the HEA and was made public. The Foundation subsequently decided that it

would not then write to the minister. Had the happy event
of finding out about the Bureau's letter not occurred,
then no doubt some respectable dental opinion would have
appeared to challenge and (who knows stop) a hard hitting
message.

There are other incidents where commercial pressures from
the sugar industry are masked as scientific opinion or
grassroots political concern to try to counter the
messages about the harmful effects of sugar but I will
not detail them here.

WHAT IS TO BE DONE ABOUT DENTAL HEALTH

It would be all too easy to contrast the power of the
sugar industry with puny forces ranged against it and
decide that nothing could be done. If so, then the
industry would have won. As an article of faith we have
to be determined that "they will not get away with it".

The first step must be to follow the leads we have as to
what will make the most difference in promoting dental
health. First we have to be clear that the most effective
means of promotion are concerned with groups of people
and areas rather than individuals. Certainly it is true
that parents and professionals such as health visitors
need to be better informed on the importance of frequency

as opposed to amount of sugar consumed. It is no bad thing to remind adults of the importance of brushing teeth to reduce gum disease. It might be useful to promote the message to grandparents and others who might wish to give children a treat that sweets are an extremely harmful present to give. Contrary to the received opinion in health education circles, all the substantial evidence suggests that hard hitting, even fear arousing messages are the most effective in producing behaviour change.[23] However it must be remembered that the public health approach must be the main thrust.

Clearly the fluoridation of water is a measure which will have the greatest benefit to the most vulnerable, who are the children of working class parents. The effects of fluoridation are to reduce or abolish class differences in the prevalence of dental caries. The provision of more dentists in areas where there are few would also be likely to produce a levelling up of the take up of dental treatment.[24] Banning the advertising of sweets on TV or at least controlling the worst excesses would help to reduce the pernicious influence on children. Regulations to prevent supermarkets displaying sweets at child level at the check out counters would reduce the level of consumption.

To achieve such measures will require a good deal of

health education, directed not at parents and non
parenting adults but at those who make the decisions
about public health measures: the politicians, the
broadcasting and advertising regulatory bodies, the
supermarket and the managers of workplaces (including
sadly hospitals and health centres) which allow sweets
and confectionery to be sold and promoted on their
premises. The difficulty is that it is not clear where
the money would come from for such health education.

The first answer would have to be that money is not
everything, that prestige can be worth much. In Britain
there has been a remarkable success story in reducing
smoking prevalence from over 50% in 1973 to less than 33%
by 1986. That achievement occurred in a period where the
health education budget against smoking was less than a
hundredth of that spent by the tobacco industry in
advertising. I believe that the effect was achieved
mainly by the authoritative pronouncements from the
medical establishment (beginning in 1962 in the UK with
the first Report of the Royal College of Medicine and in
1964 the Surgeon General's report in the USA) that
smoking can kill.

I know of chest physicians who have campaigned tirelessly
against the tobacco industry and of health promotion
professionals who have gathered and distributed evidence
on the pernicious effects of the subtler forms of

advertising. It is up to the dental profession to do the same in regard to dental health. The message may be less dramatic but needs forceful and regular repeating that sugar is bad for your dental health. To be effective the profession will need to improve its skills in political campaigning and lobbying.

Bodies such as the British Dental Health Foundation will have to be educated to become politically more shrewd and not be subtly or not so subtly swayed by the industry. For example the Foundation's leaflet on diet (sponsored by the industry) suggests that the substances causing tooth decay are "fruits, vegetables, cooked starch products, some dairy products, natural or processed foods (note the generality!), cakes, biscuits and confections plus juices and soft drinks". The statement is generally true, if remarkably non-specific, but the ordering of the list is remarkable to say the least.

The processes of persuasion can be subtle as one minister once explained in regard to practices of the tobacco industry in entertaining prominent politicians. Patrick Jenkin, an opposition front bench politician, who later became minister of health was entertained at the Glyndebourne Opera. Interviewed by investigative journalist Peter Taylor[25] he explained "I'm never somebody who likes to make war on people. If I can get

what I want by ear stroking then that is what I will do".
Asked if his ear might have been stroked he said "It
might have been...You may say my ear was stroked and I
was persuaded on the advertising 'switching brands' issue
[that is that advertising encourages brand switching not
more smokers] ... I may have been overpersuaded. But
that's certainly one of the points which the companies
made to me early on, and I took the point."

As this example shows, it is important to get the timing
right in lobbying. In the words of one rugby coach, you
must "get your retaliation in first." It is too late to
try to persuade a minister once he is in power and made
up his mind. It is important to get to him before he
knows much about the issues, at a time when he can be
persuaded. In the same way it is important to plan for
future events. The Sugar Bureau did so when it planned a
multi-million advertising campaign to coincide with
publication of the COMA report mentioned earlier.

The dental profession in its campaigning will need to
link with its natural allies. I wonder for example how
many community dentists have subscribed to The Food
Magazine or are affiliated to the London Food Commission.
There are consumer organisations such as Which? in
Britain or the International Organisation of Consumer
Unions which certainly have been supportive in regard to
anti-smoking campaigns.

There is some comfort in the maxim that "If you cannot beat them you can join them" which after all the reasoning behind this present conference. There are commercial interests which can be persuaded to join with health interests to mutual benefit. The Health Education Council, disbanded and its Director General sacked for being too political by the government, did join forces to help commercial bakers promote higher fibre and lower salt bread. The Heart Beat Wales campaign has joined with farming interests to promote lower fat milk and meat. It would be possible for the dental profession to help support attractive alternatives to sugar-laden sweets.

It should be said that those concerned with dental health must be very clear in their thinking to avoid the subtle blandishments of the industry, such as those which lured the Dental Health Foundation. The maxim applies that "He who would sup with the devil, needs must use a long spoon."

There is a need to avoid a holier than thou attitude to those who make their money from making and selling foodstuffs. None of us are free from the taint of compromise in regard to how we are paid and how we live, unless of course we live in a cave and live off wild produce, never using any of the services of the modern state. On the other hand there are so many ways in which

health educators can find themselves bound by many
invisible threads of compromise. There are orchestras and
ballet companies in Britain which have accepted
sponsorship from the tobacco industry since no harm can
come of supporting such worthwhile activities and few of
the patrons would smoke. However when suggestions are
raised that tobacco sponsorship of sport be banned, there
are many powerful and influential people who will
campaign against such a measure.

Thus education has to be an important part of promoting
dental health but what is needed is something other than
what is conventionally referred to as health education. A
schooling in the wicked ways of the world and in the
methods of Machiavelli and of Sun Tzu as outlined in The
Art of War (with its maxim of using the enemy's strength
against him) would seem to be more appropriate. As Sun
Tzu has said, by taking advantage of situations, you can
as it were, set a ball in motion on a steep slope. "The
force applied is minute but the results are
enormous."[26]

REFERENCES

1. The Guardian. 22.8.90

2. World Almanac, 1989. New York, Pharos Books, 1990,
    1-923.

3. Marmot, M. and Davey Smith, G., BMJ., 1989, **299**,
    23 Dec., 1547-51.
4. Health Service International, 1987.

5.   McCord, C. and Freeman, H.P., Excess Mortality in
     Harlem, N. Eng. J. Med., 1988, **322**, 173-177.

6.   Whitehead, M.,   The Health Divide, The Health
     Education aaaa Authority, London, March 1987.

7.   Marmot, M., Social inequalities in mortality. In
     Class and Health, ed. R.G. Wilkinson, Tavistock,
     London, 1986, pp. 21-33

8.   Haan, M., Kaplan, G.A. and Camacho, T., Poverty and
     Health. Am. J. Epid., 1987, **125**, 989-98.

9.   Whitehead, M., op. cit., p 24.

10. Mossey, J.M. and Shapiro, E., Self rated health.
     Am. J. Publ. Health, 1982, **72**, 800-08.

11. Townsend, P., Phillimore, P., and Beattie, A.
     Health and Deprivation, Croom Helm, London, 1988, 97

12. Byrne D.S., Harrisson, S.P., Keithley, J.
     and   McCarthy,   P.   Housing   and Health,   Gower,
     Aldershot, 1986.

13. Blaxter, M.,   Health and Lifestyles, Tavistock,
     London, 1990.

14. Pill N.C.H.,   and   Roisin, N.C.H.,   Prevention
     procedures and practice. Soc. Sci. Med., 1985,
     21, 975-83.

15. Murray J.J., The Prevention of Dental Disease, OUP.,
     Oxford, 1983.

16. LeGrand, J., Inequalities in Health: The Human
     Capital Approach, LSE Welfare State Discussion Paper,
     No. 1, 1985.

17. Insight Social Research, Evaluation of Poster
     Campaign in North West Regional Health Authority,
     January, 1990.

18. Ledwith, F. A survey of the impact of the NW RHA
     campaign on Health Visitors, March, 1990.

19. Child Poverty Action Group, Poverty: The Facts 1990.

20. London Food Commission, The Food Magazine, Consumer
     Checkout, April-June 1990, pp13-15.

21. Ledwith, F. Does tobacco sports sponsorship on television act as advertising to children? Health Education Journal, **43**, 85-88, 1984.

22. The Independent, 19.10.89.

23. Sutton, S.R. Fear-arousing communications. In Social Psychology and Behavioural Medicine, ed. J.R. Eiser, Wiley, Chichester, 1982, pp.303-38.

24. O'Mullane D.M. and Robinson, M.E. The distribution of dentists and the uptake of dental treatment, Commun. Dent. Oral Epidem., 1977, 5, 156-9.

25. Taylor, P., Smoke Ring, The Politics of Tobacco, Bodley Head, London, 1984, pp. 199-20.

26. Sun Tzu, The Art of War. OUP, London, 1990, p95.

THE SWISS ASSOCIATION FOR "TOOTH-FRIENDLY" SWEETS
(THE SYMPADENT ASSOCIATION)

THOMAS IMFELD* and BERNHARD GUGGENHEIM**
* Dept. of Preventive Dentistry, Periodontology and Cariology
** Dept. of Oral Microbiology and General Immunology
Zurich University Dental School
Plattenstrasse 11, CH-8028 Zurich, Switzerland

ABSTRACT

Previous speakers in this Symposium have emphasized the direct relationship between diet and the formation of dental caries. The consumption of fermentable carbohydrates results in the production of acids by dental plaque bacteria which in turn causes a demineralisation of dental hard tissues. Frequent carbohydrate ingestion results in repeated acid attacks which lead to carious lesions. Preventive cariology has primarily focussed on the protection of teeth with fluorides and on the removal of plaque by oral hygiene measures. Another preventive approach, namely diet modification reducing the frequency of consumption of acid-producing carbohydrates has not yet gained enough attention. This preventive measure can best be implemented by making available a wide variety of snacks which are non- or hypo-acidogenic. Such "tooth-friendly" confectionery designed to replace traditional sugar containing analogues can be made using sugar substitutes and intensive sweeteners. These materials have been discussed by previous speakers. This paper presents a model system, the Sympadent Association, initiated and currently used in Switzerland for developing, evaluating and promoting the use of "tooth-friendly" foods that do not give rise to intraplaque acid production. Based on the success of the Association in Switzerland an international expansion of this model is well on its way.

DENTAL CARIES, A FOOD-RELATED DISEASE

The relation between the consumption of sweet foods and the occurrence of dental disease was already known to ancient civilisations. The acid-decalcification theory, however, was first described in 1890 by W.D.Miller who established the fundamentals of modern cariology in his book "The microorganisms of the human mouth". Since then scientific evidence has mounted that dental caries is a multifactorial and basically infectious bacterial disease with complex interactions between host factors, bacterial plaque on the tooth surfaces, food consumption and time. Dental caries is a food-related disease, it is, however, not a nutritional disease because, with the exception of the caries-reducing effect of systemic fluoride, there is little if any evidence that nutrition, aside from influencing teeth during their development, plays any significant role in caries etiology. There is nevertheless abundant convincing evidence that foods exert their destructive environmental effect on erupted teeth before being swallowed and metabolized. The human diet made up by all sorts of food is the decisive source of nutrients of the oral flora. Dietary mono- and disaccharides are preferably metabolized by many plaque bacteria and starch can be degraded to maltose by salivary and bacterial amylases. Carbohydrates need not be immediately metabolized, they can be stored in the form of intra- or extracellular polysaccharides. Anaerobic fermentation of dietary carbohydrates by plaque bacteria leads to an accumulation of organic acids inside the plaque layer and thus on the tooth surface. The increased hydrogen ion concentration in plaque following each intake of fermentable carbohydrates leads to a demineralisation of the dental hard tissues. Nearly neutral pH-values of a resting (fasting) plaque provide periods of no acid attack where salivary minerals can even remineralize acid etched tooth surfaces. If the acid attacks outweigh these periods of remineralisation by frequency, duration or both the surface demineralisations will proceed to subsurface carious lesions (white-spots) and finally to cavitation of the tooth surfaces.

Caries consequently is the result of the interaction of three principal elements, i.e. susceptible teeth, bacteria (dental plaque) and diet (carbohydrates, especially sucrose). The necessity of a direct contact of diet with the teeth for the development of caries has been proved by Kite et al. (1) who showed that tube fed animals developed no caries. The predominant role of dietary carbohydrates in tooth decay has been established by Haldi et al. (2) who found active caries in animals fed only the carbohydrate component of the diet by mouth and the remainder diet by tube. Similar experiments have recently been reported by Bowen et al. (3). That bacteria are necessary in the triad of caries etiology has been demonstrated by Orland et al. (4) in gnotobiotic (germ-free) animals that developed no caries when fed a diet which produced active caries in control animals having a normal oral flora.

That plaque formed in the absence of diet differs from that formed under normal conditions and fails to lower the pH appreciably upon sugar addition has been shown in animals (5) and in man (6, 7, 8, 9).

CARIES PREVENTION BY DIET MODIFICATION

Based on the above mentioned triad of elements involved in caries etiology, efforts aiming to reduce caries incidence have emphasized the protection of dental hard tissue, the elimination of plaque and diet modification. Theoretically an optimal preventive effect would be attained by concomittant equal efforts along all three lines. Historically, however, the strongest efforts have been made for the protection of the teeth by the promotion of fluoride both collectively by means of water and salt fluoridation and individually by way of toothpastes, mouth washes, sealants and so forth. Information of the general public about the caries preventive effects of plaque removal by tooth brushing and flossing has only started later and showed less dramatic results since the success of such activities naturally depends on the personal conviction and active participation of every single individual. The third line of prevention, namely diet modification by provision of detailed sound dietary advice is only pursued since a few years and has certainly not yet yielded half the benefits that it could possibly account for. There are different reasons for this still unsatisfying situation, the most obvious being: {1} In contrast to collective fluoridation performed by the communities and to oral hygiene performed by the public, the dental profession, i.e. every single practicing dentist has to be involved by giving convincing individual dietary advice. This is not easily achieved since the dental profession and the public's perception of dentistry were (and are) generally geared to symptomatic therapy rather than to fighting the causes of dental decay. Traditionally the dentist was some kind of a "piece-worker" paid by number of fillings, crowns or number of periodontally treated teeth. The patient did not expect to get and the dentist was not trained to give dietary advice. There was and still is a widespread doubt if dietary recommendations would in any case change a patient's food consumption, especially his consumption of sweets. It is also often thought that a relatively small reduction of the daily sugar consumption will have little or no effect on dental health against the background of fluoride and oral hygiene. {2} Dietary counseling is often wrongly set equal to a simple general prohibition of sugar, a prohibition very easy to establish but very difficult to adhere to. In order to be really effective, dietary recommendations must in fact be given individually, they must be tailormade for the very patient and be firmly based on the individual dental anamnesis and clinical diagnosis. Another factor often forgotten is that dietary advice must be preceeded by a dietary analysis. In practice, how shall advice be given without knowing what a person eats, why he or she eats this or that and when and how frequently?

Since the publication of the Vipeholm study in 1954 (10) it has been accepted that the caries promoting effect of dietary sugar is more depending from the frequency of consumption than from the total amount of sugar consumed. More recently, Rugg-Gunn et al. (11) concluded from a two-year longitudinal study that sugar consumed in the form of sweets was more strongly related to caries increment than total dietary sugar.

We have undisputedly lived a great decline in caries prevalence on an epi-demiological scale, and especially a decline of smooth surface and fissure caries attributable to fluoride and oral hygiene measures. Interdental areas, however, still remain caries-prone sites of the dentition. Why ? Only a very small part of the population is able and willing to perform a perfect oral hygiene with daily thorough plaque elimination from the interdental spaces. It is civilisation to own dental floss, it would be culture, however, to really use it. Since obviously it is the real world that the average person always has plaque layers on the interdental areas, it becomes important to reduce the frequency of consumption of acid-producing carbohydrates. This preventive measure can best be implemented on a large scale by making a wide variety of snacks available which are not fermented and consequently do not give rise to acid formation in dental plaque. Such confectionery products can be manufactured by replacing sugar with synthetic or natural non-nutritive intensive sweeteners and/or with nutritive sugar alcohols (polyols), so-called sugar substitutes.

METHODS FOR EVALUATION OF THE CARIOGENIC POTENTIAL OF FOODS

The idea to reduce the cariogenic challenge by providing the consumer with a group of snack foods which are not harmful to teeth requires both a definition of the cariogenic potential and methods for assessing this cariogenic potential of foods. The cariogenicity of a food can only be established in experiments on humans producing real carious lesions. As investigations with human subjects such as the Vipeholm study (10) are no longer considered ethically feasible, it became necessary to develop model systems to predict the cariogenic risk associated with the consumption of different foods. Such indirect methods establish a cariogenic potential without regard to actual consumption patterns. Accordingly, the cariogenic potential is defined as a food's ability to foster caries in humans under conditions conductive to caries formation.

Three main methods have been developed. The first approach, based on Stephan's (12) idea of introducing electrometric methods for intraoral pH-measurements in 1940 is the assessment of acid production in dental plaque. This technique has undergone many refinements reviewed elsewhere (13, 14, 15). A second model is relying on animal experiments usually performed on rats eating test foods under controlled feeding conditions (16). A third model category is based on enamel demineraliz-ation/remineralization systems. The latter two methods have recently been reviewed (17).

In 1985 an international scientific consensus has been reached with regard to methods to be used to evaluate the cariogenic potential of foods. A key component of this consensus developed by more than 70 scientists from 8 countries was that plaque-pH-telemetry from interproximal sites is a method which will allow, in human volunteers, unequivocal demonstration of the non-acidogenic or hypo-acidogenic nature of a specific food (18). The consensus statement from the report (19) was as follows: "Each of the three types of methods (plaque sampling, touch electrodes, interproximal telemetry) will satisfactorily identify non-acidogenic foods when used properly with appropriate positive (sucrose) and negative (sorbitol) controls. When one is testing substances which can potentially deposit on the plaque surface, thereby influencing the readings made at this plaque surface, one must make measurements at the inner plaque surface." The above Consensus Conference also defined the aim of assessments of the cariogenic potential of foods. Such assessments should be sufficiently valid and practical to be of direct use to consumers, dental health care personnel, food producers and other interested groups. On the basis of the state of the art it was further concluded that a categorization of foods as having no or low cariogenic potential was sufficient. It is obvious that this categorization placed emphasis on foods that are to be recommended rather than on foods identified as potentially harmful. It was equally pointed out that the testing should focus. largely on ready to eat foods. The latter two points were adopted in view of the positive experiences made in Switzerland since 1969 when the oral health-related food label "safe for teeth" was first authorized by the Federal Health Authorities.

THE SWISS ASSOCIATION FOR "TOOTH-FRIENDLY" SWEETS

The background of the Sympadent Association is a unique and fascinating story in caries research that has evolved from the pioneering work of Professor Hans R. Mühlemann in Zurich, Switzerland. As early as 1964 Mühlemann started to seriously search for a method to assess the cariogenic potential of foods. The most convenient methods for monitoring in situ changes of human dental plaque-pH after the ingestion of food already available at that time involved either the sampling of plaque for extraoral measurement or the insertion of touching electrodes into plaque covering the teeth. These methods only allowed measurements from readily accessible tooth surfaces and it was thought that their predictive value depended on the extent to which pH-changes in such areas really mirror those in plaque on more caries-prone sites of the dentition. In the very same year Kleinberg and Jenkins (20) reported that the pH of fasting and non-fasting plaques in different areas of the mouth, assessed with antimony probing electrodes, varied according to intraoral location. They found that plaques on interdental contact areas due to poor access of saliva and to food retention exhibited the lowest fasting and non-fasting pH values. They concluded that the regional distribution of plaque pH was in good correspondence with the generally described pattern of caries incidence that ranks contact areas along with pits and fissures as highest at risk. Mühlemann decided that a method aiming to give clinically relevant dietary advice should consequently be able to quantitate intraplaque acid production in areas exhibiting the highest risk of damage, i.e. interdentally. He thus became responsible for the development of a unique biotelemetry system which was later named "intra-oral plaque pH-telemetry" (21, 22, 23). Oral appliances containing miniaturized indwelling glass pH-electrodes were prepared for human volunteers. The ion-sensitive tips of the electrodes were so placed as to directly reside in an interdental space opposing the interproximal area of an adjacent natural abutment tooth. These test prostheses with clean pH-electrodes were inserted and the subjects were asked not to alter their eating habits. With the single exception of water rinses, they were bound to refrain from all oral hygiene measures. The prostheses were not removed during the test periods, thus allowing an undisturbed growth of interdental plaque over the tips of the interdentally oriented electrodes. The hydronium ion concentration under an undisturbed layer of interdental plaque could thus be continuously monitored in vivo during and following food ingestion. The measurements did not disturb food consumption nor the normal diffusion of substrates into the interdental areas and plaque. The neutralizing effect of salivary buffers as well as eventual alkalinization of acidified plaque by buffers added to manufactured products could be adequately assessed in a natural environment. Intraoral telemetry and its applications were continually documented

(24, 25, 26, 27) and the method was described in detail and critically reviewed in 1982 and 1983 (28, 29). Its reproducibility was assessed in longterm retrospective studies comparing the findings after administration of standard sucrose rinses in volunteers over periods of 2 to 5 years. The consistency of the results proved to be excellent (30, 31, 32). A comparison of pH-telemetric findings after equal carbohydrate exposure in children, adolescents and adults supported the extrapolation of results of adult volunteers to the average consumer (33).

Through a series of pioneering studies Mühlemann and co-workers demonstrated that foods could be divided in two classes: Minimally acidogenic or hypoacidogenic products of which there were few, and acidogenic products which represented the majority of the foods tested. Based on these observations Mühlemann appropriately directed his attention towards the development of snacks that would not harm the teeth. He became an early promotor of the replacement of sugars by sugar substitutes and was able to convince two Swiss and an American confectionery producer to start developing such products. This direct industrial application of research findings turned out to become the initiation of a whole range of new products and of a completely new market segment. Before, however, it got so far, Mühlemann's determination to actively apply scientific academic insights for the promotion of oral health in the public made him approach the Swiss Health Authorities. It was due to his endeavours that already in 1969 the Swiss Office of Health introduced a legislation for the labelling of manufactured foods and drugs with regard to dental health in order to identify low caries risk dietary components for the consumers. Based on article 185i, paragraph 2, of the Swiss Food Ordinance (Schweizerische Lebensmittelverordnung, LV) products can be labelled "safe for teeth" (German: "zahnschonend", French: "ménageant les dents") if they have been proved in intraoral plaque pH-telemetric tests not to depress the pH of interdental plaque below 5.7 by bacterial fermentation either during consumption or up to 30 min later. Advertising a product as "non-cariogenic" or "less cariogenic" ("nicht kariogen", "non cariogène" or "weniger kariogen", "moins cariogène") is only allowed when based on a long-term clinical caries test in man. The use of the term "anticariogenic" ("antikariogen", "anticariogène") is not allowed because it suggests a therapeutic effect and may invite abuse. The label "safe for teeth" as used in the Swiss Food Ordinance was the first and only food regulatory action known that allowed the consumers to exclude a caries risk when selecting foods, snacks, beverages and drugs.

Despite his remarkable scientific and political accomplishment the initial sales volume of "safe for teeth" confectionery products was lower than Mühlemann had anticipated. This was apparently due to the fact that the palatability and the price of the new products did not yet match their sugar sweetened competitors. Further of importance was that the legal status of polyols and intensive sweeteners with regard to basic clearance, to restrictions for dosage, limitations of distribution and mandatory special labelling varied between different countries. This lack of unanimity even within the EEC inhibited free import and export of "safe-for-teeth" confectionery thus diminishing economies of scale and therefore discouraging the interest of many a multinationally operating firm. Most important, however, was the lack of product promotion and advertizing. The Swiss population, unfamiliar with health-related food labelling at that time, was not aware of the significance of "safe-for-teeth" products for their dental health. Mühlemann's unbroken efforts were rewarded on July 6, 1982, when a joint action called "Aktion Zahnfreundlich" between Swiss University Dental Institutes and industry was designed and initiated to propagate chewing gums, snacks and sweets labelled "tooth friendly". In spite of the great enthusiasm of the Swiss Dental Schools it took more than two years of difficult negotiations before the campaign obtained the full support of industry. The reasons for the hesitancy on the part of the involved companies appeared to be a lack of confidence in the possibility to increase sales with statements related to dental health and even more important it was hard for them to surpass the strong psychological barrier to collaborating with competing corporations.

These initial problems in initiating and expanding this system devoted to increase the public awareness, understanding and utilisation of "tooth friendly" products have since long been overcome. "Aktion Zahnfreundlich" (The Sympadent Association) was legally registered as a non-profit association with members from the Swiss University Dental Schools, manufacturers of sweeteners and sugar substitutes and producers of "safe-for-teeth" confectionery. A public relations agency was then employed to develop an organised campaign. A pictograph (Fig. 1) showing a smiling tooth protected by an umbrella was selected through an open competition and the Sympadent Association now owns trademark rights for it in many countries. All confectionery and similar sweet foods that comply with the above mentioned Swiss food regulation for "safe-for-teeth" products qualify for distinction by the smiling tooth pictograph. Against payment of a royalty the members of the Sympadent Association obtain the right to exhibit the pictograph on the wrapper of their accordingly tested products. With the royalty fees the association runs nation-wide public information programs explaining the meaning of the pictograph and the oral health benefits of the products exhibiting this sign. The Board of the association and the Secretary work honorary. Strategies and activities of the association are yearly discussed and agreed upon in a General Assembly. Initially an explanatory text was developed and the emblem propagated primarily through paid advertisements. More than 100 feature articles appeared in Swiss newspapers and magazines. Radio interviews were held and brochures distributed by practising dentists and dental school representatives. Large posters were place in supermarkets and a special promotion for children was made at the Swiss National Circus. During 1985 and 1986 a TV-spot was broadcasted in the three national languages.

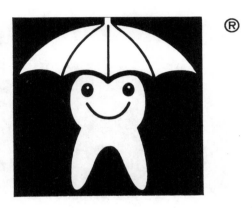

Figure 1. Pictograph of the Sympadent Association

The unique success of this approach was illustrated when four years after the foundation of the association, in fall 1986, an independent market research company was commissioned to investigate the level of public awareness for "tooth friendly" products. Their representative consumer survey showed that about 80% of the Swiss population and more than 90% of children were fully aware of the significance of the "happy tooth" pictograph and were informed about the oral health benefits of the associated products.

Of equal importance was that market data showed a continuous remarkable growth of the sugar substituted segment of the Swiss confectionery market (Fig. 2). Sales of such products (sweets, chocolate and chewing gum) have increased from 1400 tons in 1981 to 3500 tons in 1989, when they represented 17,9% of the total market (Fig. 3). In the same year 86% of sugar substituted confectionery products carried the "happy tooth" pictograph. The average daily consumption of such products in Switzerland can be calculated to be more than 1,4 g per capita.

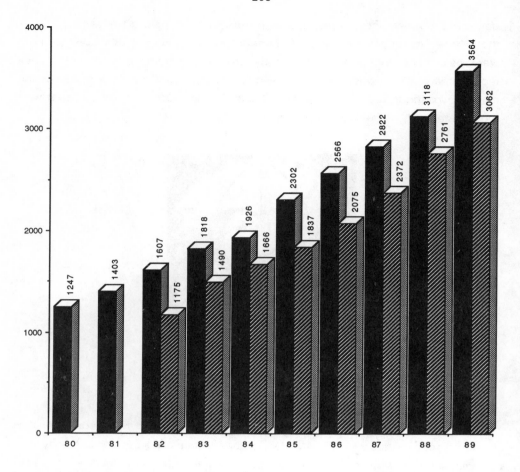

Figure 2. Sales figures (in tons) of sugar substituted confectionery products in Switzerland from 1980 to 1989.

■ total sugar substituted confectionery products

▨ sugar substituted products registered with the Sympadent Association and carrying the pictograph

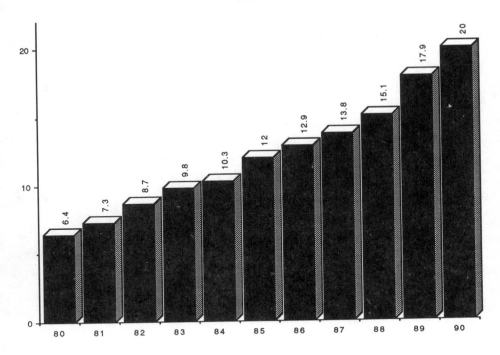

Figure 3. Sales volume of sugar substituted confectionery products in per cent of the total market in Switzerland from 1980 to 1989 and 1990 (projected).

The success of the Sympadent Association in Switzerland did not go unnoticed by the neighbouring countries. Following the Swiss example a sister association was founded in Germany in 1985. The German association has meanwhile assembled over a dozen members from industry, part of them already being members of the Swiss association. An increasing number of German products now show the "happy tooth" pictograph on their labels. A French association has been founded in 1989 and the French Health Authorities have signalled their interest in this matter. It is equally asthonishing to look at export figures of member industries into countries that do not (yet) have an own association. A growing sales volume of confectionery bearing the pictograph of the association is found in over 15 countries reaching from nearby Italy to far Hongkong.

FUTURE PROMOTION OF "SAFE-FOR-TEETH" SWEETS

From the viewpoint of preventive dentistry and aiming to decrease caries prevalence by diet modification an international expansion of the Swiss model is imperative. The present time seems ideally suited to try and implement this goal (34): There is a growing consumer interest in a healthy lifestyle and nutrition is perceived more than ever as a way to improve the quality of life. The demand for correspondingly labelled products is great and professional dietary recommendations are widespread in the media. The realisation of a Common European Market in 1992 is yet another opportunity to try and get broader recognition of the Sympadent Campaign. In the US the FDA has recently reexamined its formerly very restrictive policy concerning health-related claims on food labels.

The long-term goal of an international association must be to reduce the cariogenic challenge to the human dentition by providing the consumer with non-acidogenic alternatives for the traditional sugar containing foods.

REFERENCES

1 . Kite O.W., Shaw J.H., Sognnaes R.F., The prevention of experimental tooth decay by tube feeding. J Nutr, 1950, **42** , 89-100.

2 . Haldi J., Wynn W., Shaw J.H., Sognnaes R.F., The relative cariogenicity of sucrose when ingested in the solid form and in solution by the albino rat. J Nutr, 1953, **49** , 295-306.

3 . Bowen W.H., Amsbaugh S.M., Monell-Torrens S., Brunell J., Kuzmiak-Jones H., Cole M.F., A method to assess cariogenic potential of food-stuffs. J Am Dent Assoc, 1980, **100** , 677-681.

4 . Orland F.J., Blayney J.R., Harrison R.W., et al., Use of the germfree animal technique in the study of experimental dental caries. I. Basic observations on rats reared free of all microorganisms. J Dent Res, 1954, **33** , 147-174.

5 . Bowen W.H., Metabolic criteria indicative of cariogenicity in primates. Proceedings ERGOB Conference, In: Health and Sugar Substitutes, Guggenheim Ed, Karger, Basel, 1979, 235-240.

6 . Littleton N.W., Carter C.H., Kelley R.T., Studies of oral health in persons nourished by stomach tube. I. Changes in the pH of plaque material after the addition of sucrose. J Am Dent Ass, 1967, **74** , 119-123.

7 . Littleton N.W., McCabe R.M., Carter C.H., Studies of oral health in persons nourished by stomach tube. II. Acidogenic properties and selected bacterial components of plaque material. Arch Oral Biol, 1967, **12** , 601-609.

8. Cooke V., Petropolou K., Mandel I.D., Ellison S.A., Falcetti J., Trieger N., Plaque in tube-fed persons. I. Metabolism and chemistry. J Dent Res, 1982, **61**, (Spec Iss A), 250.

9. Ellison S.A., Cooke V., Mandel I.D., Trieger N., Falcetti J., Plaque in tube-fed persons. II. Microbiology. J Dent Res, 1982, **61**, (Spec Iss A), 250.

10. Gustafsson B.E., Quensel C.E., Swenander Lanke L., et al., The Vipeholm dental caries study. Acta Odontol Scand, 1954, **11**, 232-364.

11. Rugg-Gunn A.J., Hackett A.F., Appleton D.R., Jenkins G.N., Eastoe J.E., Relationship between dietary habits and caries increment assessed over two years in 405 English adolescent school children. Arch Oral Biol, 1984, **29**, 983-992.

12. Stephan R.M., Changes in hydrogen-ion concentration on tooth surfaces and in carious lesions. J Am Dent Assoc, 1940, **27**, 718-723.

13. Edgar W.M., Geddes D.A.M., Plaque acidity models for cariogenicity testing - Some theoretical and practical observations. J Dent Res, 1986, **65**, (Spec Iss), 1498-1502.

14. Geddes D.A.M., Newman P., Impact of technology - Plaque-pH methods., In: Foods, Nutrition and Dental Health, vol. 5, Hefferren, Koehler and Osborn Eds., Pathodox Publisher, Park Forest South, 1984.

15. Schachtele C.F., Jensen M.E., Comparison of methods for monitoring changes in the pH of human dental plaque. J Dent Res, 1982, **61**, 1117-1125.

16. König K.G., Schmid P., Schmid R., An apparatus for frequency controlled feeding of small rodents and its use in dental caries experiments. Arch Oral Biol, 1968, **13**, 13-26.

17. Clarkson B.H., In vitro methods for testing the cariogenic potential of foods. J Dent Res, 1986, **65**, (Spec Iss), 1516-1519.

18. DePaola D.P., Executive summary. J Dent Res, 1986, **65**, (Spec Iss), 1540-1543.

19. Schachtele C. and members of the working group, Human plaque acidity - working group consensus report. J Dent Res, 1986, **65**, (Spec Iss), 1530-1531.

20. Kleinberg I., Jenkins G.N., The pH of dental plaques in the different areas of the mouth before and after meals and their relationship to the pH and rate of flow of resting saliva. Arch Oral Biol, 1964, **9**, 493-516.

21. Graf H., Mühlemann H.R., Glass electrode telemetering of pH changes of interdental human plaque (Abstract). J Dent Res, 1965, **44**, 1139.

22. Graf H., Mühlemann H.R., Telemetry of plaque-pH from interdental area. Helv Odontol Acta, 1966, **10**, 94-101.

23. Mühlemann H.R., Intra-oral radio telemetry. Int Dent J, 1971, **21**, 456-465.

24. Imfeld T., Mühlemann H.R., Cariogenicity and acidogenicity of food, confectionery and beverages. Pharmacol Therapeut Dent, 1978, **3**, 53-68.

2 5 .   Imfeld T., Mühlemann H.R., Evaluation of sugar substitutes in preventive cariology. J Prev Dent, 1977, **4** , 8-14.

2 6 .   Imfeld T., Evaluation of the cariogenicity of confectionery by intra-oral wire telemetry. Schweiz Mschr Zahnheilk, 1977, **87** , 437-464.

2 7 .   Mühlemann H.R., Sugar substitutes and plaque-pH-telemetry in caries prevention. J Clin Periodontol, 1979, **6** , (Extra Iss), 47-52.

2 8 .   Imfeld T., Interdental plaque-pH-telemetry. Proceedings of a workshop on saliva-dental plaque and enamel surface interactions, In: Surface and colloid phenomena in the oral cavity: Methodological aspects. Frank and Leach Eds., IRL Press, London, 1982, 143-156.

2 9 .   Imfeld T., Identification of low caries risk dietary components. Monogr Oral Sci, 1983, **11** , 1-198.

3 0 .   Imfeld T., In vivo assessment of plaque acid production, a long-term retrospective study. Proceedings ERGOB Conf. Geneva 1978, In: Health and sugar substitutes. Guggenheim Ed., Karger, Basel, 1979, 218-223.

3 1 .   Firestone A.R., Imfeld T., Schiffer S., Reproducibility of in vivo interdental plaque-pH measurements in humans following a sucrose rinse. Caries Res, 1985, **19** , 189-190.

3 2 .   Firestone A.R., Imfeld T., Schiffer S., Lutz F., Measurement of interdental plaque-pH in humans with indwelling glass pH electrode following a sucrose rinse: A long-term retrospective study. Caries Res, 1987, **21** , 555-558.

3 3 .   Imfeld T., Lutz F., Intraplaque acid formation assessed in vivo in children and young adults. Pediatr Dent, 1980, **2** , 87-93.

3 4 .   Baer A., Significance and promotion of sugar substitution for the prevention of dental caries. Lebensm Wiss u Technol, 1989, **22** , 46-53.